A CRISIS OF REPUBLICANISM

A CRISIS OF REPUBLICANISM

★

AMERICAN POLITICS IN THE CIVIL WAR ERA

★

EDITED BY LLOYD E. AMBROSIUS

★

UNIVERSITY OF NEBRASKA PRESS

LINCOLN & LONDON

The paper in this book meets
the minimum requirements of
American National Standard for
Information Sciences—Permanence of
Paper for Printed Library Materials,
ANSI Z39.48–1984.

Library of Congress Cataloging-in-Publication Data

A Crisis of republicanism: American politics in the Civil War Era /
    edited by Lloyd E. Ambrosius.

        p.   cm.

    Includes bibliographical references.

    ISBN 0-8032-1026-4 (alk. paper)

1. United States – Politics and government – 1849–1877.

2. Republicanism – United States – History – 19th century.

3. Political culture – United States – History – 19th century.

4. Political parties – United States – History – 19th century.

5. United States – Politics and government – 1845–1849.

I. Ambrosius, Lloyd E.

E415.7.C79   1990

320.973'09'034 – dc20   89-38372

                        CIP

FOR JAMES A. RAWLEY

Carl Adolph Happold Professor Emeritus of History,

University of Nebraska — Lincoln

CONTENTS

INTRODUCTION

★

LLOYD E. AMBROSIUS

American politics during the Civil War era experienced a crisis of republicanism. At stake were the fundamental values and characteristic institutions of the United States. Neither the leaders nor the voters could escape this crisis involving their national identity. Presidents, political parties, and the people themselves all wrestled with the crucial issues that shaped this era. Defining their future within the context of their heritage, Americans confronted the meaning of their history and destiny. This crisis of republicanism thus revealed the qualities of American political culture in the nineteenth century.

Consensus and conflict coexisted in the political culture of the United States. Accepting a broad consensus of republicanism, which affirmed both liberty and equality, Americans nevertheless disagreed with each other over the government's legitimate functions. Some, in the tradition of Alexander Hamilton, favored a positive role for the government in promoting economic development and preserving social order. The Federalist and then the Whig political parties, and still later the Republicans, adopted this perspective. Others, following Thomas Jefferson, preferred to limit the government's role and, distrustful especially of national power, emphasized states' rights. The early Republican and subsequent Democratic parties took this view. Even within parties, conflict arose over socioeconomic and ethnocultural differences, sometimes resulting in political realignment. When, as in the 1850s, partisan realignment was also sectional, it served as a harbinger of the nation's division between the North and South. During the Civil War era, as at other times, political parties evidenced what Bernard Sternsher labeled "conflict within consensus."[1]

Continuity and change also characterized American politics. Within

the framework of the Constitution, political institutions afforded remarkable stability in a dynamic society. In the 1830s, the two-party
system became a permanent feature in the United States, shaping the
nature of its republican government on the national, state, and local
levels. The two-party system has continued into the 1980s, despite
obvious changes in the twentieth century. As James L. Sundquist observed, "There has been an extraordinary degree of institutional continuity through all the changes. The basic two-party system has prevailed with only occasional brief interruptions for fifteen decades. . . .
The unique setting in which American parties operate—a single elected
chief executive, a federal governmental structure that translates itself
into a federal party structure—is basically unchanged."[2] Given this
remarkable continuity, the crisis of republicanism in the Civil War era
can provide a historical perspective on controversial political agendas of
recent years.

Ambivalent in their republicanism from the American Revolution
onward, leaders and citizens of the new nation typically regarded their
political culture as at once unique and universal. Contrasting their
republic with the monarchies of Europe, they emphasized the differences between the New and Old Worlds. They sought cultural as well as
political independence and endeavored to isolate the United States
from the corrupting influence of Europe. Still, Americans offered their
experience in self-government as a model for the entire world. They
proclaimed its freedom, despite the continuing existence of the "peculiar institution" of slavery. Denouncing European colonial empires,
while creating an imperial republic for themselves, they pursued what
Jefferson called an "empire of liberty." Even if it required the removal of
American Indians, the enslavement of African-Americans, the subor-
dination of Hispanic-Americans, and the exclusion of Asian-Americans,
the creation of a republican empire fulfilled their mission as defined by
the dominant Anglo-Americans. Paradox and irony, even hypocrisy,
characterized the political culture of the United States.

American republicanism originated from the legacies of early modern Europe, which the English, in particular, had transplanted to the
New World. J. G. A. Pocock and Sacvan Bercovitch have traced the roots
of American political culture back to the Renaissance in Machiavelli's
Florence and to the Protestant Reformation in England. Thus the politi-

cal thought that distinguished the United States, they noted ironically, was not unique to the New World but a contribution of the Old. In America, as in Europe, the intertwining of political theory and theology had created a symbiotic relationship between patriotism and religion. The Atlantic republican tradition and the Puritan jeremiad had joined by the time of the American Revolution to produce a new national consciousness, at once secular and sacred. The result was what Pocock called "the Americanization of virtue" and Bercovitch described as "the typology of America's mission."[3]

Republicanism furnished the political consensus not only for leaders of the American Revolution and framers of the Constitution but also for subsequent generations. Pocock agreed with Bernard Bailyn and Gordon S. Wood in emphasizing the contribution of the radical Whigs or Country party in England during the eighteenth century to the emerging American revolutionary ideology. He, too, rejected the "Lockean consensus" in American political thought. Republicanism experienced recurrent crises, with the Revolution as the first in the series, and remained fragile in the United States. Its success was no more certain here than it had been in Florence during the original Machiavellian moment. Constant vigilance was needed to protect public virtue against corruption. Consequently, as Pocock observed, "the Americans, having made the republican commitment to the renovation of virtue, remained obsessively concerned by the threat of corruption—with, it must be added, good and increasing reason. Their political drama continues, in ways both crude and subtle, to endorse the judgment of Polybius, Guicciardi, Machiavelli, and Montesquieu in identifying corruption as the disease peculiar to republics: one not to be cured by virtue alone."[4] The crisis of republicanism during the Civil War era was such a moment in the drama of American politics.

In the United States, definitions of republicanism changed as new conditions altered traditional ideas. For the American revolutionary elite, republican government required balancing the three orders in the social hierarchy (the one, the few, and the many) with the different forms of government (monarchy, aristocracy, and democracy). But by renouncing England's monarchy and its hereditary aristocracy, revolutionary ideology undermined this conception of republicanism. Appealing to the people's sovereignty to justify independence in 1776, the

American gentry found it increasingly difficult thereafter to legitimate any form of government other than democracy. Their idea of "natural aristocracy" was not, over the long run, a viable justification for restricting power to an elite in an egalitarian society. Both monarchy and aristocracy succumbed to the increasingly democratic republicanism of the United States. Although American leaders, and especially presidents, continued to come from privileged social backgrounds, they embraced the new democratic ethos by promoting the "log cabin myth."[5]

The emergence of a market economy also altered the American definition of republicanism. This economic development challenged the earlier conception held by the radical Whigs or Country party that commercialism might corrupt republican government. In that view, to preserve public virtue, republican citizens needed to retain economic independence, based on ownership of freehold property. From that classical perspective, republicanism was well suited to an agrarian society but potentially incompatible with capitalism. It was more Jeffersonian than Hamiltonian. Therefore, the commercial and industrial development of the United States posed fundamental questions about the very existence of the American republic. "Throughout the nineteenth century," observed William L. Barney, "Americans engaged in an ongoing debate over how best to reconcile the emerging market society with their political culture of republicanism." Eventually, despite their lingering doubts, they embraced capitalism along with democracy. "Much more so than in Europe, *democracy* and *capitalism* very nearly became synonymous terms in the United States. As long as white males apparently had an equal chance to compete, making money and pursuing liberty meant the same thing, and most Americans continued to believe that they lived in a classless society."[6]

This identification of democracy and capitalism with republicanism transformed American political culture by the eve of the Civil War. Freedom now meant popular choice and individual opportunity for economic mobility, not the careful balancing of power in a hierarchical society. It was equated with private gain rather than public virtue. Robert H. Wiebe aptly called this transformation "the opening of American society." It was, he stressed, dependent on the seemingly limitless space of the North American continent. It also exacted a high price from its victims. "The democratization of American society," he observed, "coincided with the strengthening of the slave system, the drive to exterminate native Americans, and the establishment of a class line. An opening for some meant a cruel closing to many others. The same society that encouraged its members to disperse throughout a vast domain made the issue of expansion a justification for division and war. Yet a distinctive American society did appear, however ambiguously; a democracy did develop, however brutally; and a national expansion did occur, however costly in lives." The limits felt by the gentry of the revolutionary republic no longer restricted the democratic society. "In the hands of the new democracy," Wiebe noted, "progress was an awesome two-edged sword indeed. One side cut the way to an extraordinary vision of human potential: perfectionism. The other side hacked down the people who were obstructing that vision: genocide."[7]

In the American political culture of democratic republicanism, which had emerged by the mid-nineteenth century, Anglo-Saxon racism prevailed. White Americans, who defined the "manifest destiny" of their providential nation, identified its progress with racial Anglo-Saxonism. Science offered theories to promote this popular prejudice regarding superior and inferior races. In both the North and South, the political ideology of racial destiny of the Anglo-Saxons justified the westward expansion of the United States at the expense of the Indians and Mexicans. "By the 1850s," as Reginald Horsman explained,

the American sense of idealistic mission had been corrupted, and more of the world's peoples were condemned to permanent inferiority or even to extinction. General world progress was to be accomplished only by the dominating power of a superior race, and a variety of lesser races were accused of retarding rather than furthering world progress. A traditional colonial empire had been rejected, but it was believed that the expansion of a federal system might ultimately prove possible as American Anglo-Saxons outbred, overwhelmed, and replaced 'inferior' races. This time was to be hastened by commercial penetration of the most distant regions of the earth. The commercial endeavors of a superior people were confidently expected to transform the world while bringing unprecedented power and prosperity to the United States.[8]

Racism became identified with democracy and capitalism in the nation's republican political culture.

The crisis of republicanism during the Civil War era arose from the tensions inherent in American political culture. Conflict within consensus eventually precluded a peaceful resolution of differences between the North and South. Analyzing the political crisis of the 1850s, Michael F. Holt emphasized the common republican ideology that had shaped the two-party system: "It is not too great an oversimplification to say that since 1776 the essence of American politics had been the battle to secure republicanism—government by and for the people, a government of laws whose purpose was to protect the liberty and equality of the people from aristocratic privilege and concentrations of tyrannous power." Northerners and southerners shared the anxiety that the corruption of republican government could result in tyranny or slavery. "It is of the utmost importance in understanding the events of the 1850s, therefore, to recognize that the word 'slavery' had a political meaning to antebellum Americans quite apart from the institution of black slavery in the South. It implied the subjugation of white Americans to another's domination. It meant the absence of independence. It was the antithesis of republicanism." From this republican perspective, northerners reacted against the South's assertiveness during the controversy over the Kansas-Nebraska Act, perceiving a threatening Slave Power conspiracy. "Thus," Holt continued, "opposition to the Nebraska Act and the Slave Power conspiracy provided a cathartic opportunity to restore to political activity its basic purpose, to regain a sense that vigilant citizens could save republican government." Northerners reacted to protect themselves and their democratic republic, which they regarded as essential to their future welfare as free citizens. "What was ultimately at stake in the sectional conflict was the enslavement of white Americans in the North by despotic slaveholders bent on crushing their liberties, destroying their equality in the nation, and overthrowing the republican principle of majority rule." Paradoxically, southerners shared similar concerns. They, too, understood their situation within the context of republican political culture. As Holt noted, "The pervasive presence of black slavery was a constant reminder to whites that they must be ever vigilant in the defense of republicanism."[9] The crisis of the Civil War era revealed conflict between the North and South within their republican consensus.

American political culture contained contradictions. The North and

South, and to some extent even the West, represented "alternative Americas." The war, culminating in the Union's victory over the Confederacy, eventually resolved the conflict over these alternative definitions of American nationality. As Anne Norton observed, the Puritan legacy in the form of the "American jeremiad"—as Bercovitch described it—profoundly shaped northern, but not southern, political culture. Puritans had turned into Yankees by the nineteenth century. Their ideal of America was expressed in the vision of a providential republican empire. "The partisans of this empire were charged with a duty to posterity," Norton explained. "The expansion of the temporal boundaries of the nation to include remembered forebears and an imagined posterity was accompanied by a constriction of the cultural boundaries of the nation. American republicanism was, this articulation affirmed, the consequence of the Reformation. American nationality thus required a corresponding reformation of the immigrants. They were obliged to adopt 'Anglo-Saxon' mores and the tenets of the Protestant religion prior to becoming truly American." Southern political culture, in contrast, adhered to the classical republicanism of the eighteenth century, as described by Pocock. In the South, where agriculture remained dominant, a Country-party form of republicanism still furnished a critique of capitalism. Southerners were Cavaliers, not Puritans or Yankees. These differences in republican ideology separated the South from the North. As Norton noted, "Southerners of widely varying views on black slavery were united among themselves by their agreement that nature was the proper determinant of political status. This belief, while it did nothing to resolve the issue of slavery, changing it merely to a debate over the natural rights and requirements of the two races, distinguished the South from the North, where political and personal status were determined by election and by law and where the question of rights fell before that of duties entailed on members of the divinely or temporally covenanted community."[10] Contradictions within antebellum republicanism divided the United States into culturally distinct regions. The Civil War between the North and South pitted these "alternative Americas" against each other on the battlefield.

Victory by the Union over the Confederacy enabled the northern alternative of republicanism ultimately to prevail in the United States. The dominant political culture, which Abraham Lincoln had epitomized and which embraced democracy and capitalism, eventually succeeded in defining the nation's destiny. In the reconstructed nation, despite continuing conflict, this new republican consensus shaped the Americans' understanding of the Civil War experience. Most American historians also accepted this perspective. Before the mid-twentieth century, as David W. Noble observed, historians shared with others a Progressive paradigm. Their interpretations of the unique role of the United States in world history expressed this distinctively American ideology. They emphasized, accordingly, the contrast between the Old and New Worlds and the republican virtue of their nation. This belief in American exceptionalism, which had characterized the revolutionary ideology of the new republic's founders in the eighteenth century, influenced historical writing in the nineteenth and early twentieth centuries. Among others, George Bancroft and later the Progressive historians Frederick Jackson Turner and Charles Beard perpetuated the typical perspective of American political culture.[11]

Ironically, argued Noble, following Bercovitch and Pocock, the ideas that Americans regarded as distinctively their own had originated in the Old World during the Renaissance and Reformation. The Puritans had brought with them a progressive conception of time and had affirmed the metaphor of two worlds. They had anticipated the possibility of predicting and controlling the future. The founders of the United States, though drawing on that Reformation tradition, had also incorporated into their revolutionary ideology the theme of republican virtue from the civic humanists of the Renaissance. American political culture in the nineteenth century, as well as historical writing, expressed the European legacy from both of these sources.

After World War II, as the culmination of an intellectual process that had started in the 1890s, American historians developed a new Counter-Progressive paradigm to replace the previous Progressive perspective. They offered what became known as the Consensus approach in the 1950s. Richard Hofstadter and Louis Hartz, along with theologian Reinhold Niebuhr and others, searched for new understandings of their nation's past and of its place in the world. They stressed continuity and deemphasized conflict in the American experience. In their interpretations, both democracy and capitalism shaped the public policies of the United States at home and abroad, regardless of which leaders or political parties were in office. The tradition of republican virtue as a critique of capitalism, which Beard had reiterated, now seemed irrelevant to Niebuhr and Hofstadter. Moreover, these scholars rejected the historic belief in American exceptionalism, or the metaphor of two worlds, while still seeking a way to characterize the American political tradition and to distinguish it from Soviet Russia's in the Cold War era.[12]

Moving beyond consensus by the 1960s, American historiography evidenced a variety of new approaches. Some historians—such as J. G. A. Pocock, Sacvan Bercovitch, and Anne Norton—used literary sources in creative ways to reassess American political culture. They focused primarily on ideology. Others—such as Thomas B. Alexander, Allan G. Bogue, Joel H. Silbey, and Michael F. Holt—contributed to the "new political history." Shifting the emphasis to behavior, these scholars adapted from the social sciences both new theoretical conceptions and new methodologies employing quantification. Rather than concentrating on elite leaders, they devoted their attention to voting patterns in legislatures and general elections. They studied ethnocultural factors in American politics, in contrast to the focus on political economy that had characterized the Progressive historians. Still others—such as William Appleman Williams and other New Left historians—continued to devote their attention to socioeconomic issues but within the context of American political culture. All of these approaches tended to produce interpretations with greater sensitivity toward outsiders, whether racial and ethnic minorities, women, or other marginalized persons in the United States and in other countries.[13]

These new approaches to American history have opened possibilities for reinterpreting American politics during the Civil War era. The chapters in this volume, examining both ideology and behavior, reveal the contradictions of American political culture. Employing the methodologies of traditional and new political history, the different authors explore the contributions of leaders and voters. The elite and the people interacted in the American republic to create a complex pattern of conflict within consensus and change within continuity. The authors study the political behavior of obscure voters and prominent leaders to clarify their ideological or moral commitments as well as their material or practical interests. These scholars see both cultural diversity and economic rivalry as having shaped the nation's political choices, challenging not only the political parties but the constitutional system of republican government. The outcome of the Civil War determined whether the founders' legacy could be preserved and how the United States would be reconstructed. This crisis shaped the future of American republicanism.

The following chapters, like American historiography generally since the 1960s, recognize the necessity of simultaneously explaining the American republic's distinctive characteristics and the internal conflict and discontinuity in its history. Using various approaches, the authors seek to disclose the rich diversity as well as the unifying dimensions of American history. The conflict between the North and South, climaxing in the Civil War, revealed that all Americans did not share identical ideals and interests despite their common heritage of the Revolution. Alternative definitions of republican ideology intertwined with ethno-cultural and socioeconomic factors to shape the pattern of American politics. Many of the ideological and behavioral conflicts stemmed from European legacies. Americans lived in a transatlantic world. Despite their political independence in 1776, they had not achieved cultural isolation from the Old World. Although they shared a political culture of republicanism in the nineteenth century, differences of race, ethnicity, and religion as well as class and economics divided them into rival political parties and sections. For this reason, the following interpretations examine conflict and change, along with consensus and continuity, in American politics during the Civil War era.

Using the quantitative methodologies of new political history, Thomas B. Alexander focuses on the Free Soil party of 1848 as the harbinger of the collapse of the second two-party system. In agreement with Joel H. Silbey, who emphasized the "partisan imperative"[14] in American politics during the mid-nineteenth century, he acknowledges the loyalty of voters to the Whig and Democratic parties. He seeks to explain why some of them voted for the Free Soil ticket and whether the reasons for defection in 1848 heralded the political realignment of the 1850s. By studying voters' behavior, Alexander endeavors to reveal the ideological as well as material interests of the electorate. He concludes that the Free Soil party strengthened its political appeal beyond that of the Liberty party in 1840 and 1844 by attracting voters from the two major parties. The Whigs lost support especially in Ohio, Indiana, and

Michigan, though more Democrats defected in New England, Pennsylvania, and Illinois, as well as New York, where the Free Soil presidential candidate, Martin Van Buren, carried his Democratic faction into the new party. Alexander shows that a self-interest in western lands, especially in northern areas not enjoying agricultural prosperity, combined with a symbolic commitment against slavery to attract voters to the Free Soil party. The ticket expanded its appeal beyond the abolitionists, who had supported the Liberty party earlier. The Republican party, which emerged in the aftermath of the Kansas-Nebraska Act and in the midst of nativism, enjoyed a still broader appeal. Attracting northern Democrats as well as Whigs, the Republicans succeeded by identifying their party with the free-soil cause, which was by the late 1850s even more of a symbolic issue. It offered northern voters an opportunity to reject the Slave Power conspiracy of the South, while incidentally protecting their own self-interest in the West. To some extent, then, the 1848 presidential election was a harbinger of the realignment of the 1850s. Alexander concludes that the final collapse of the second two-party system came with the nativist movement and the antislavery reaction against the Kansas-Nebraska Act. These new developments brought substantial changes in American politics which were only partly foreshadowed by the Free Soil party of 1848.

In his chapter on Salmon P. Chase, John Niven offers a biographical sketch of an outstanding leader in the antislavery movement before the Civil War. He focuses on the political elite rather than on the electorate. As Niven reveals, Chase combined a genuine antipathy toward slavery with personal ambition as a politician. He wanted to restrict slavery to the southern states, excluding it from federal territories as well as northern states. According to his interpretation of "freedom national," the Constitution empowered Congress to adopt this free-soil position, as the republic's founders had done with the Northwest Ordinance. The Ohio politician began his career as a Whig, switched to the Liberty and then Free Soil parties, and eventually joined the Republicans. He sought to broaden the appeal of these parties—and of himself as a candidate—beyond the antislavery cause. Catering to the economic and nativist interests of Democrats and Know-Nothings, he won election as United States senator and Ohio governor. His subsequent failure to win the Republican nomination for president in 1856 and 1860 revealed

Chase's difficulty in balancing moral considerations with self-interest at a time of intense socioeconomic and ethnocultural conflict. Niven attributes this failure to the flaws in Chase's personality and character. His treachery alienated his erstwhile and potential political allies. Like Viscount Bolingbroke, a leader of the Country party in eighteenth-century England, he warned the nation about corruption in its political system. Though he recognized the Slave Power threat to republican government, Chase lacked the personal qualities that might have enabled him to make a greater contribution to liberty for either black or white Americans. He was not the Republicans' choice to lead their party and the nation during this crisis of republicanism.

Instead, Abraham Lincoln provided the leadership to preserve the Union and emancipate the slaves. According to Phillip S. Paludan, Lincoln developed a particular style of political rhetoric during the Civil War to achieve these substantial goals. He used "conversation" as a means of reconciling the inherent conflict between the twin legacies of the American republic's founders: the Declaration of Independence and the Constitution. Lincoln sought to fulfill the Declaration's promise of equality while preserving the constitutional system, which had permitted slavery in the southern states. He articulated a new consensus, with both liberty and law, to heal the warring nation. Earlier in his career, as lawyer and politician, Lincoln had employed the adversarial style of argument. Partisanship in politics and evangelical zeal in religion had encouraged this rhetorical form in the United States. During the Civil War, however, the president resorted increasingly to storytelling, a typically southern form of communication, as a way to reconstruct the Union under the Constitution.

Emphasizing Lincoln's southern heritage, Paludan challenges a prevalent interpretation of his place in American political culture. In contrast, Richard N. Current stressed his northern ideology: "Lincoln stood, as did the Republican party, for individual opportunity, for technological advance, for the enlarged productivity of farms and factories—all with the encouragement of the federal government. He fully shared the ideas and ideals that were implied in the party slogan of 'Free soil, free labor, free men.' He was the very embodiment of the spirit of modernization that was coming to predominate in the North. This spirit was the antithesis of the traditionalism that more and more characterized the South." Anne Norton, too, viewed Lincoln as the epitome of northern political culture. She interpreted his rhetoric as an example of what Bercovitch called the "ritual of consensus." Referring to the Gettysburg Address, she observed: "Here Lincoln, following the form of the jeremiad, finds in present affliction evidence of past and future greatness. He exhorts Americans not to seize their rights but to shoulder their duties. He articulates the vision of a temporally infinite nation, accomplishing a great task in the fullness of time. This is a Puritan speech. But there is something Western in it as well. The national reformation, this 'new birth of freedom,' is achieved through battle and death."[15] Historians such as Current and Norton believe that the Union's victory in the Civil War enabled northern political culture to prevail in the United States. Paludan, however, emphasizes the southern heritage in Lincoln's political rhetoric.

Harold M. Hyman examines Lincoln's constitutional thought within the context of northern political culture, which affirmed the Constitution and the Declaration of Independence and embraced democracy and capitalism. Along with other antislavery lawyers Salmon P. Chase, Edwin M. Stanton, and William Whiting, he advocated "freedom national" as the remedy for instability in the previously state-centered federalism. This alternative would give the national government new responsibility for protecting individuals' civil rights and liberties. The promise of equality in the Declaration of Independence could be fulfilled by extending the federal Bill of Rights to the states and local communities. For these antislavery lawyers, freedom national meant equal access under the law to property and education and generally to the rights of free citizens. Like the Northwest Ordinance earlier, the Homestead and Morrill acts implemented the ideology of these lawyers during the Civil War. As politicians and as lawyers who had worked for corporations, they identified freedom with individual rights of access. Theirs was the new conception of republicanism which had emerged in the North by the mid-nineteenth century. Out of this conception of freedom national came the Thirteenth and Fourteenth amendments, which would guarantee equal legal rights for all American citizens, whether white or black. By the war's end, Lincoln moved the nation toward racial equality as an expression of the same political values that affirmed democracy and capitalism. But freedom national was not fully realized after his assassination. Instead, Andrew Johnson's racism and his ideology of states' rights shaped the national government's role during the postwar years. Moreover, a new form of education for lawyers fostered among them a different legal culture, which undermined the Thirteenth and Fourteenth amendments, postponing Lincoln's agenda for decades. Even as late as the 1980s, the civil rights movement encountered resistance from some Republicans, who still rejected the antislavery lawyers' vision.

One major reason for the failure of freedom national was the act of an individual, John Wilkes Booth, who assassinated Lincoln. As Hans L. Trefousse observes, Booth succeeded in reversing the national government's direction by enabling Johnson to become president. Although Lincoln and Johnson were similar in certain aspects of their personal background and in their loyalty to the Union, they were different in fundamental ways. They did not share the same political outlook. As a Whig and later a Republican, Lincoln favored cooperation between government and business to promote economic development. He identified with Henry Clay's American System in the Hamiltonian tradition. Johnson, in contrast, was a Jeffersonian-Jacksonian Democrat, who opposed government interference in the economy and espoused agrarian democracy. The two presidents differed as well in their performance as executives. A shrewd politician, Lincoln steered between radicals and conservatives in his party as he moved deftly toward emancipation of the slaves and freedom for all Americans. Johnson, however, alienated so many Republicans in Congress that they eventually impeached him. Above all, Trefousse argues, attitudes toward race and slavery separated the two men. Lincoln had expressed his antislavery views long before he became president. Although he evidenced the racial prejudice so typical of white Americans during the nineteenth century, he was more liberal than most of his contemporaries. In sharp contrast, Johnson was strongly racist. A slaveowner before the war, he accepted emancipation reluctantly. His racist attitudes toward black Americans prevented the new president from seeking to fulfill the promise of equality to former slaves. His actions encouraged white southerners to resist black suffrage and other substantial changes in race relations during postwar Reconstruction. Rejection of Lincoln's synthesis of the Declaration and the Constitution, with the Supreme Court's acquiescence, prevented

African-Americans from gaining freedom national in practice until the emergence of the civil rights movement in the mid-twentieth century. That lingering problem would eventually produce another crisis of republicanism in the United States.

The following chapters focus on important aspects of American political culture in the nineteenth century. Employing the methodologies of traditional and new political history, the authors examine the elite as well as the electorate in the American republic. Their interpretations encompass conflict within consensus and change within continuity. From different perspectives, these historians provide new insights into the crisis of republicanism in American politics during the Civil War era.

NOTES

1. Bernard Sternsher, *Consensus, Conflict, and American Historians* (Bloomington: Indiana University Press, 1975), pp. 129–207.

2. James L. Sundquist, *Dynamics of the Party System: Alignment and Realignment of Political Parties in the United States* (Washington, D.C.: Brookings Institution, 1983), p. 148.

3. J. G. A. Pocock, *The Machiaevellian Moment: Florentine Political Thought and the Atlantic Republican Tradition* (Princeton: Princeton University Press, 1975), pp. 506–52; Sacvan Bercovitch, *The American Jeremiad* (Madison: University of Wisconsin Press, 1978), pp. 93–131.

4. Pocock, *Machiavellian Moment,* p. 548; Bernard Bailyn, *The Origins of American Politics* (rpt. New York: Vintage Books, 1967); Bernard Bailyn, *The Ideological Origins of the American Revolution* (Cambridge, Mass.: Harvard University Press, 1967); Gordon S. Wood, *The Creation of the American Republic, 1776–1787* (Chapel Hill: University of North Carolina Press, 1969).

5. Edward Pessen, *The Log Cabin Myth: The Social Backgrounds of the Presidents* (New Haven: Yale University Press, 1984).

6. William L. Barney, *The Passage of the Republic: An Interdisciplinary History of Nineteenth-Century America* (Lexington, Mass.: D. C. Heath, 1987), pp. 1, 88.

7. Robert H. Wiebe, *The Opening of American Society: From the Adoption of the Constitution to the Eve of Disunion* (New York: Vintage Books, 1984), pp. xv, 344.

8. Reginald Horsman, *Race and Manifest Destiny: The Origins of American Racial Anglo-Saxonism* (Cambridge, Mass.: Harvard University Press, 1981), p. 297.

9. Michael F. Holt, *The Political Crisis of the 1850s* (New York: Wiley, 1978), pp. 56, 134–35, 151–52.

10. Anne Norton, *Alternative Americas: A Reading of Antebellum Political Culture* (Chicago: University of Chicago Press, 1986), pp. 75, 130.

11. David W. Noble, *The End of American History: Democracy, Capitalism, and the Metaphor of Two Worlds in Anglo-American Historical Writing, 1880–1980* (Minneapolis: University of Minnesota Press, 1985), pp. 3–64; Richard Hofstadter, *The Progressive Historians: Turner, Beard, Parrington* (New York: Vintage Books, 1968); Richard Nelson Current, *Speaking of Abraham Lincoln: The Man and His Meaning for Our Times* (Urbana: University of Illinois Press, 1983), pp. 172–86.

12. Louis Hartz, *The Liberal Tradition in America: An Interpretation of American Political Thought since the Revolution* (New York: Harcourt, Brace and World, 1955); Richard Hofstadter, *The American Political Tradition and the Men Who Made It* (New York: Vintage Books, 1948); Reinhold Niebuhr, *The Irony of American History* (New York: Charles Scribner's Sons, 1952); Reinhold Niebuhr, *The Children of Light and the Children of Darkness: A Vindication of Democracy and a Critique of Its Traditional Defense* (New York: Charles Scribner's Sons, 1944); Sternsher, *Consensus, Conflict, and American Historians*, pp. 1–126; Noble, *End of American History*, pp. 65–114.

13. Robert Kelley, *The Cultural Pattern in American Politics* (New York: Knopf, 1979), pp. 3–28; Allan G. Bogue, "United States: The 'New' Political History," *Journal of Contemporary History* 3 (January 1968): 5–27, reprinted in Robert P. Swierenga, ed., *Quantification in American History: Theory and Research* (New York: Atheneum, 1970), pp. 36–52; Jerome M. Clubb and Allan G. Bogue, "History, Quantification, and the Social Sciences," *American Behavioral Scientist* 21 (November–December 1977): 167–85; Allan G. Bogue, Jerome M. Clubb, and William H. Flanigan, "The New Political History," *American Behavioral Scientist* 21 (November–December 1977): 201–20; Noble, *End of American History*, pp. 115–40.

14. Joel H. Silbey, *The Partisan Imperative: The Dynamics of American Politics before the Civil War* (New York: Oxford University Press, 1985).

15. Current, *Speaking of Abraham Lincoln*, p. 163; Norton, *Alternative Americas*, p. 309; Bercovitch, *American Jeremiad*, pp. 132–75.

CHAPTER ONE

★

HARBINGER OF THE COLLAPSE OF

THE SECOND TWO-PARTY SYSTEM:

THE FREE SOIL PARTY OF 1848

★

THOMAS B. ALEXANDER

One of the most pervasive scenarios in United States history textbooks, frequently embedded in chapters with such titles as "Expansion and Conflict," runs about as follows: The acquisition of vast new territory through the annexation of Texas, the seizure of Mexican lands, and the division of the Oregon country with Great Britain rejuvenated the long dormant concern with the status of slavery in territories, a concern that was never again fully quieted until it made possible the Republican party's victory that led to the Civil War. In such an interpretation, the Free Soil party of 1848 takes its place in the first presidential election that might qualify as a harbinger of the breakup of the Democrat-Whig party system. And by implication at least, the candidacy of former President Martin Van Buren elevated the third-party effort of the free-soilers to significant levels and was the first blow in weakening many voters' affective attachment to one of the major parties.

Anyone who has given even a cursory glance to the tide of recent analysis of this problem knows that the political developments from 1848 to 1856 were far more convoluted than such a presentation acknowledges. The political vitality of nativist sentiment through the Know-Nothing movement and the national American party of 1856, not to mention its impact at state and local levels, has been illuminated extensively in recent writings. Michael F. Holt, for one, has speculated that the American party instead of the Republican party might have become the second major party of the North. Regionwide and state-level studies, together with a growing library of biographies, have added much to our awareness of the often bafflingly complex maneuvering of political leaders and of their assessments of positions on issues that might attract a critical mass of defectors from the opposition or mobilize new voters.[1] I am not trying to add to our understanding of leaders; that has already been accomplished extremely well and is still being extended. Moreover, I need to make clear that I have never thought the Free Soil party provided an exact predictive formula for subsequent party realignment. I am using the word *harbinger* to mean something that merely foreshadows what is to come.

That leaders were a crucial component of the restructuring of the party system is nowhere seriously questioned. Yet they are numbered in the hundreds at most, and the Free Soil presidential vote in 1848 totaled more than 170,000 outside New York State, where Van Buren's candidacy split the Democrats almost equally and represented Democratic party factionalism more than grass-roots free-soil sentiment. I can extract very little from the election statistics for New York for my purposes and usually exclude them from my analyses. What I am seeking to understand is the composition of the voiceless mass of voters who responded to the free-soil appeal and why they did. The Liberty party vote in 1844 of more than 46,000 can be accepted as ideologically antislavery before the free-soil issue came to prominence. The some 124,000 (again outside New York) who represented additions to the earlier Liberty vote provide the element to be analyzed in seeking some educated guesses about the special importance of the free-soil appeal to the early stages of party realignment. These 124,000 were less than 8 percent of the northern vote in 1848, rendering my search uncomfortably close to the needle-in-a-haystack simile.

I am focusing narrowly on the question of what the voters' response may have been to the decision of antislavery leaders to join the Free Soil movement in 1848. In pursuing estimates about that issue, I need to draw inferences about the behavior of voters and even risk educated guesses about their possible perceptions and hence motives. Probably everything that human ingenuity can design is somewhere in the literature as inferences about these matters from the literary sources, essentially from leadership perceptions or public positions. I shall not add anything to the list of options but merely try to add weight to some as opposed to other existing assessments.

Many have argued that numerous voters perceived that their own or their relatives' self-interest in moving west required a victory for the free-soil policy, either to keep the desirable land from being engrossed by slaveowners or to keep their future homes from being socially complicated by a biracial population. Others have emphasized that containment of slavery was a symbolic and constitutional way to attack that institution in the abstract, or alternately, to attack a South that was increasingly seen as a generalized enemy. The extent of northern white prejudice against black people has repeatedly divided historians concerned with the roots of free-soil impetus among the masses. Laborers, farm or otherwise, many scholars allege, believed that their very dignity and image of self-worth would be damaged by having slaves in the vicinity doing work similar to theirs. Alarm that the political power of southerners might grow as they expanded into the territories is rarely left out of the equation, raising the specter of free men of the North falling into a kind of "slavery" to an aggressive Slave Power. These concerns, supplemented by the long-standing struggle for the right of petition in Congress, provided the peroration of the Free Soil platform: "Free Soil, Free Speech, Free Labor, and Free Men."[2] We can infer directly what the promoters of this slogan thought would affect their target audience. What can we estimate about the way that audience perceived the message?

My inferences are based on county-aggregate election and census data and arise from ecological regression of aggregate political indicators on other political indicators or on aggregate socioeconomic indicators based on published 1850 United States census data.[3] I need to explain this approach before I can hope to provide an even barely persuasive argument, for I will assume that voters' constancy to party was the overwhelming rule and that a decline in one party's share of total county vote between elections did not result from a game of musical chairs but essentially reflected defection of voters. More specifically, I accept the assumption that when the Democratic percentage of total vote remained constant between 1844 and 1848, while the Whig percentage declined an absolute 10 percent and Free Soil gained an absolute 10 percent over the 1844 Liberty party share, it was Whigs who defected to Free Soil.

Figure 1 is a scattergram image of ecological regression using all counties of the free states that were not affected by the creation of new counties between 1840 and 1844 and that have extant voting returns for both elections. These two presidential elections represent as firm a regionwide two-party alignment as can be found for the second two-party period. In assessing the meaning of this evidence of voters' constancy, I have written elsewhere: "These estimates are not intended to be taken literally as suggesting that a certain proportion of the actual individuals who voted Democratic in one election also voted Democratic in a later one. Deaths, the coming of age of prospective voters, and migrations into or out of a county preclude such literal interpretation. The . . . speedy addition of immigrants to the voting pool further becloud[s] the meaning of voter constancy estimates. . . . What a well-founded and very high estimate of continuity of voting alignment . . . does literally mean is that a party's proportion of the total vote by county is changed very little from one election to the next." Why this aggregate stability existed is not the same as whether it did, but the two are closely related. In view of numerous individual-level studies of voters' constancy in this period, surely the most parsimonious hypothesis is that "men who voted in the two elections rarely switched parties," that deaths and departures were not party-biased, "that voters coming of age commonly accepted their [families'] party preference, and that newcomers to a neighborhood were influenced by the dominant party preference there."[4]

I have been deeply impressed during the past five years with the potential impact on county-aggregate election analysis of our ever-growing awareness of the great mobility of people in these years. The remarkable flow of migrants not only into but through counties, stopping to vote perhaps only once or twice before moving on, can be

Figure 1. Party Continuity in Presidential Elections, 1840–44

X = Democratic party percentage of total vote by county, 1840
Y = Democratic party percentage of total vote by county, 1844
r = .92; R^2 = .84; $\underline{a}$ = 9.08; $\underline{b}$ = .86; standard error of estimate = 4.14
N = 433 (all counties of the North not affected by creation of counties from 1840 through 1844)
Least-squares estimate of continuity ($\underline{a} + \underline{b}X$ where X = 100) = 95%

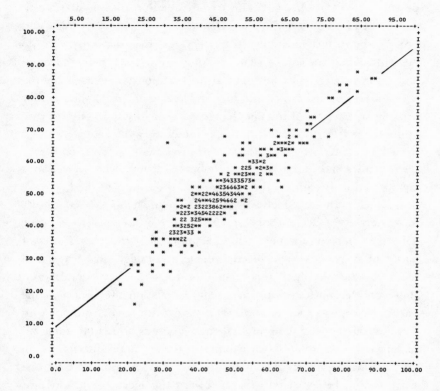

illustrated for a few localities where poll books for a number of successive years have survived, though we have only scattered fragments from
which to generalize. Nonetheless, conceiving of a county as a place
where the longtime residents voted far more often than the transients
during a decade and perhaps competed with each other for influence
with the new or temporary voters—where the stayers, in other words,
dominated the political complexion of the county yet had to cope with a
sometimes torrential stream of migrants—brings some significant assumptions to bear on ecological regression.[5] The movers probably had
lower turnout rates, but there is evidence that many voted once or twice
before moving on. We know so little about internal migration in the

United States in the 1840s and 1850s that we are necessarily groping in the dark here.

In Figure 1, the regression line does not run from corner to corner but begins at 9 percent at the left margin (the intercept) and ends at 95.5 percent at the right margin. This is interpreted as a least-squares estimate that in a county with zero Democratic vote in 1840 we would predict 9 percent Democratic vote in 1844, and that in a county with 100 percent Democratic vote in 1840 we would predict 95.5 percent Democratic vote in 1844. The continuity estimate is important in itself, but the least-squares estimate of continuity and the intercept value together provide an estimate of the net change between elections—in this case approximately 4.5 percent increase, $9 - (100 - 95.5)$.[6]

Such estimates are biased for at least three reasons. The first is simple: counties had widely varying numbers of voters. The correction is equally simple: weight by the total vote in the county at the first election, which in this case increases the estimate of Democratic continuity to 96 percent (4 percent loss) and lowers the estimate of Democratic gain to 6.5 percent, for a net gain of 2.5 percent. The second source of bias, I am increasingly convinced, is the effect of migration. States with many counties that had large changes in total vote between elections show considerably less county-aggregate correlation levels between one party's percent in each election than states with fewer counties with large changes in county-level total vote. There is no readily apparent pattern to the volatility. To the extent that migration produced random fluctuations in party shares of total vote, counties dominated by one party should be expected to shift toward the mean, or toward less extreme domination in the second of two elections. Referring to Figure 1, counties in the lower third of Democratic strength in 1840 might well appear somewhat lower in Democratic strength in 1844, while counties in the highest third of Democratic strength in 1840 might be somewhat higher in 1844 in that proportion if random volatility had not been introduced by migration. Adjusting estimates for such bias would raise the level of continuity and lower the level of gain, and I am increasingly convinced that such an adjustment approximates the reality we are seeking.[7]

The third source of bias is from other kinds of random variance presumably exogenous to the political arena we are considering. For one thing, the slope of the line is affected by the presence of outlier cases that may result from errors in recording data. The county represented by the point farthest from the line, above and to the left, is Hancock County, Illinois, where the Whigs won with 72 percent of the vote in 1840 but lost to the Democrats two and four years later when the Democrats had about 70 percent of the vote. There is a strong probability that the returns in 1840 were accidentally reversed.[8] The general point is that random variation tends to change values toward the mean or, resorting to amateurish imagery, brings up the values in the lower range and brings down the values in the higher range—in effect, reducing the steepness of the slope and contributing to an impression of lower continuity and higher switching than is justified.

The closeness of fit to the line is reflected in the correlation coefficient (in this instance .93 weighted by county-level total vote in the first election). Another important measure is the standard error of estimate, which in this weighted regression instance is 3.26 percent. It is probably more than coincidence that this 3.26 average error in prediction is very close to the percentage of those switching parties for purely personal reasons discovered in twentieth-century survey research.[9] This scattergram picture of the regression is a benchmark, I think, against which to measure the predictability of the second of any pair of elections in this period.

This brings us to one final consideration I need to clarify before offering the results of my analyses. It is popular in research on recent elections to seek to consider mobilization along with party alignment, speaking of the way nonvoters in one election behaved in the next and the proportions of voters in the first election from each party who did not vote in the second election. This approach is now frequently used for elections of the mid-nineteenth century, but for many reasons I cannot be comfortable with the implicit assumptions.[10] We rarely have registration lists as a basis for computing turnout, and for most states the voting pool is not perfectly measurable even statewide, not to speak of the county level, because of the incessant population mobility. I much prefer to treat the ever-changing ecological unit, a county, as a place where one party's standing appeal is best reflected in the proportion of the total vote it draws in each election, without attempting to estimate who might have left the county or arrived there and who entered or departed from the voting lists.

Now, we can turn to the Free Soil vote of 1848 and seek an overview of its distribution, using as a universe the northern (free state) counties excluding New York State. The Free Soil ballot was evidently available almost everywhere in 1848. Only 7 percent of these counties had not a single presidential Free Soil vote, yet almost one-fourth of the northern counties reported fewer than twenty votes and half of them fewer than one hundred. Regional distribution was extremely uneven.[11] In New England almost one-fifth of the total vote was Free Soil; in the Old Northwest (Ohio, Indiana, Illinois, and Michigan) the Free Soil share was 11 percent; in New Jersey and Pennsylvania it was less than 3 percent.

Mobilizing new voters was often mentioned by participants as a political tactic accounting for much of the Free Soil vote. This view has appealed to many historians as well. Examination of county-aggregate data does not substantiate such a view. Plotting change in turnout between 1844 and 1848 against the Free Soil percentage of the total vote by county shows that greater Free Soil success was almost never associated with increased turnout and, for the five states to be used intensively in this study (Pennsylvania, Ohio, Indiana, Illinois, and Michigan), was more common in counties with decreased turnout. In Ohio, which will be found to be anomalous, an unusual decline in turnout occurred, and the highest Free Soil success was in counties with very substantial declines. For the entire North exclusive of New York State, the greater Free Soil success occurred in counties with decreased turnout or those with little change in turnout between 1844 and 1848. It may be argued, of course, that previous voters abstained and were replaced by previous nonvoters attracted by the Free Soil appeal, but I think the burden of proof rests with the advocates of such a scenario.

In New York State, Democratic party factionalism almost completely determined the share received by the Free Soil party. Even outside New York, however, the impact of rivalry, even bitterness, between Martin Van Buren's followers and those of Lewis Cass almost certainly influenced Democratic defection rates. For this reason, in seeking some clues to which voters were attracted by the free-soil principle, separating the sources of Free Soil acquisitions in 1848 into Democratic or Whig offers better promise. Using the percentage loss by each party between the 1844 and the 1848 elections as the basis for estimating the Free Soil appeal separately by party reveals an extremely erratic pattern.[12] In New England the Democrats' mean county loss to Free Soil was above 20 percent, but the Whigs' loss was only 10 percent. New Jersey had only one county in which the Free Soil party gained substantially over the Liberty party vote in 1844. Defections to Free Soil in Pennsylvania were almost all from Democratic ranks; in Ohio the reverse was the case. Relative defection rates in Indiana were similar to those of Ohio. Illinois and Michigan counties provided evidence of considerable defection from both parties but with contrasting relative rates: in Illinois, an 18 percent mean county Democratic rate but only 7 percent Whig; in Michigan, only a 6 percent Democratic rate but 18 percent Whig. Even in New England there were substantial distinctions among the individual states in the sources of Free Soil gain over Liberty shares of the total vote.[13]

A state-level inspection of the estimated sources of Free Soil acquisitions discloses some evidence that local political leadership had a profound effect on whether it was Democrats or Whigs who shifted—or significant numbers of both. Candidates' strategy is generally recognized as an important influence on voters' decisions to switch to another party. In Pennsylvania the Free Soil appeal was obviously directed selectively at Democrats; the reverse was true in Ohio. Examining county-level sources of Free Soil acquisitions provides a clear illustration of the critical importance of local Free Soil leaders' party alignment. For more than half of the approximately three hundred counties with even one-half of 1 percent Free Soil vote, the estimates are that essentially all of the aggregate shift was from the ranks of one party—the Democratic party in slightly more than one-fourth and the Whig in another fourth of the counties. Democrats and Whigs were nearly equal sources of Free Soil gains over Liberty party shares of the total vote in only about one-sixth of these counties. One receives the impression that Free Soil activists within a single county were commonly effective in one but not the other major party.

Figure 2 offers a visual impression of this erratic pattern. The A part of the figure is a map display of the Illinois counties with at least one-

Figure 2. Party Shares of Estimated Loss to the Free Soil Party of 1848 in Excess of Loss to the Liberty Party of 1844 in Presidential Elections Mapped by County for All Counties with at Least 0.5 Percent Free Soil Vote

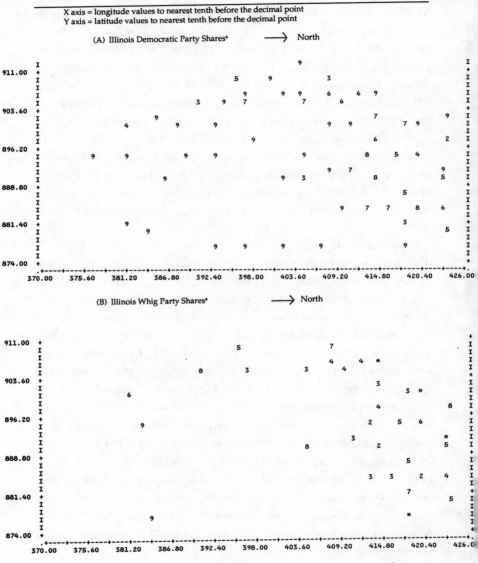

*Numbers are deciles of share, percentages rounded to nearest tenth. 100 percents included in 9s; 10 percents printed as *s; less than 5 percent results in a zero value that erases the county from the map. Therefore, a 9 for one party may appear on the corresponding map as either an * or missing.

Figure 2 (*continued*)

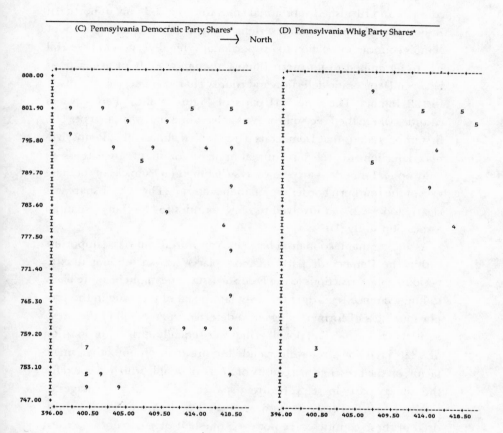

(C) Pennsylvania Democratic Party Shares[a]   ⟶ North   (D) Pennsylvania Whig Party Shares[a]

half of 1 percent Free Soil vote in 1848. The top map shows relative Democratic contributions to the total of Free Soil gains over the 1844 Liberty party vote.[14] Counties coded 9 are those in which the Democratic share of switchers was closest to 90 percent. The single 2 in the northern tier of counties is where the Democratic share was closest to 20 percent. A glance at the map just below (B), which portrays the distribution among counties of the Whig share, reveals an 8 in the same county. A 9 on either one of these mirror-image maps may be matched by an * (= 1), or a blank space if the other party's share was closer to 100 percent than to 90 percent. With this information, it is simple to observe the distribution of the separate parties' contributions. Democrats were the major source of defections in many counties in every part of the state. Whigs made the major contributions in only four southern Illinois counties and furnished substantial votes for Free Soil only in northern Illinois. For this reason, any serious analysis of the characteristics of Illinois counties in relation to proportional Whig defection to Free Soil has to be limited to northern Illinois, though a study of associations between Democratic defection and county characteristics may be made for all Illinois. The C and D parts of Figure 2 show Pennsylvania counties where the Free Soil vote was at least one-half of 1 percent. The first impression is that Democrats (C) provided almost all of Pennsylvania's defections to Free Soil but that in many counties there was essentially none. Democrats are shown as switching in most parts of the state except the southern border region in the interior. The Whigs' share was clearly too weak and involved too few counties to be of any use in an association study (D).

Assuming that factionalism between Van Buren and Cass supporters within the Democratic party in most places was so influential as to becloud voters' reactions to the Free Soil issue, one might be more likely to find evidence regarding the popular appeal of the issue in the proportional loss of former Whigs who defected to Free Soil in the presidential race in 1848. Yet not all Whigs were equally at risk. The location of 1848 Free Soil strength depended, more than on any other single factor, on the presence in a county of a core of people who had voted for the Liberty party in 1844. Figure 3 is a scattergram of percentages of total vote in 1844 (Liberty) and 1848 (Free Soil). More than one hundred of these counties gave not even one-half of 1 percent to a third party in either election. The imposed line of equality of percentage for X and Y illustrates that for only two counties was the Free Soil proportion less than the Liberty proportion, and for one of those counties the Liberty party won only 2 percent of the vote. The regression line indicates that the Free Soil vote was on average almost two and one-half times that of the Liberty party. Inverting the regression yields an estimate that more than one-fourth of the Free Soil vote came from Liberty party supporters. Although there was some Free Soil vote in almost one hundred counties that registered no Liberty vote, only one-fourth of these (twenty-two counties) recorded more than a 5 percent Free Soil

Figure 3. Association of Liberty Party Vote of 1844 with Free Soil
Party Vote

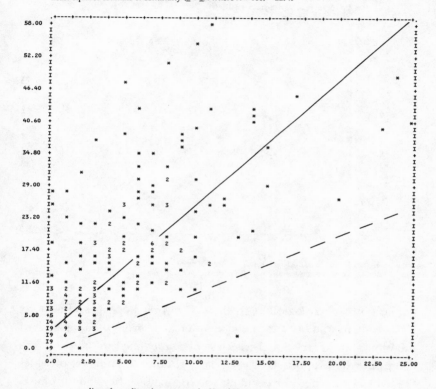

X = Liberty party percentage of total vote by county, 1844
Y = Free Soil party percentage of total vote by county, 1848
r = .79; R² = .63; a =3.29; b =2.25; standard error of estimate = 6.97
N = 411 (all counties of the North not including New York State that were not affected by creation of
    counties from 1844 through 1848)
Least-squares estimate of continuity (a + bX where X = 100) = 229%

—— —— —— = line of equality of percentage for X and Y
More than nine cases may belong in any cell with "9" because of the single digit maximum in the
    SPSS Scattergram procedure. In this figure, the cell for "0" - "0" has far more than nine cases.

proportion of total vote. It is necessary, therefore, to acknowledge that
efforts to use county-level ecological regression in searching for hints of
voters' perceptions, even among Whigs who switched parties, is handi-
capped by the biasing effect of prior Liberty party strength.

The Whig sources of Free Soil strength were substantial in New
England but erratic from state to state. Regrettably, there are too few
counties in a single New England state to justify any confidence in the

Figure 4. Estimates of Whig Party Proportional Loss to the Free Soil
Party of 1848 between the Presidential Elections of 1844 and 1848
Mapped for All Indiana Counties with at Least 0.5 Percent Free Soil Vote

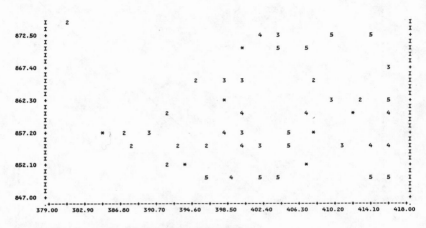

X axis = longitude values to nearest tenth before the decimal point
Y axis = latitude values to nearest tenth before the decimal point

implications of ecological regression. Our best hope lies elsewhere.
Ohio, Indiana, Illinois, and Michigan offer some promise for analysis of
the Whig shift to Free Soil. Inspection of county maps in these states to
determine the proportion of each party shifting to Free Soil provides
the evidence needed for deciding where analysis offers any promise.
Figure 4, for example, reveals that in Indiana, counties throughout
most of the state provided a range of Whig defections from 1 to above
19 percent, though many southern counties showed little Whig loss. If
we accept the limitations imposed by Democratic party factionalism,
analysis of Democratic shifts in Pennsylvania and Illinois will be useful.
Underlying the Democratic tidal wave to Free Soil in New York was a
distribution of Whig defections across much of the state that is at least
worth examining, although nothing of interest has been uncovered.

One way to test the probability that local economic and demographic
circumstances in a county predisposed voters to be sensitive to Free Soil

concerns as a self-interest issue is to compare the geographic sources of Free Soil acquisitions with some indicators that could be related to voters' perceptions. Because the nativist and "Free Labor" concerns become involved, the list of regressor variables from the 1850 census begins with the percentage of foreign-born in the total population and includes the percentage of adults employed in manufacturing, though neither category provided unambiguous evidence. Eleven indicators for which the values might reasonably be associated with plans or hopes for moving on to new lands, or expectations that the next generation might, are shown on Table 1.

In addition, the latitude of the county is employed because so much evidence exists that distance from slave states is related to growing strength of all forms of antislavery perception. This consideration does, indeed, so affect measures of association between political and economic attributes that sometimes it is necessary to control for latitude in the lower tier of free states. The strengths and forms of association with latitude, as inspected on scattergrams, being generally asymmetrical and rarely close to linear and often complicated by extreme values, strongly argue against partial regression analysis. Moreover, the controlled association is unlikely to be any more linear and hence not usefully interpretable from product moment partial coefficients. Separate examinations of the southern and northern halves of these states have served as a straightforward control.[15]

Scattergrams by state, or by portions of a state, with the county as the unit of observation, for each of the census variables with proportional Whig loss or, as appropriate, proportional Democratic loss to Free Soil provide the basis for addressing the question, What were the characteristics of counties in which voters seemed most susceptible to the Free Soil appeal? The measure of political response is the proportion of voters at risk who are estimated to have defected to Free Soil, defined as the absolute percentage decline for one party as a proportion of its percentage of the total vote.[16] A glance at the resulting ninety-eight scattergrams (one for each of seven geographic areas for each of fourteen indicators) yields two impressions: there are very few high linear correlations, and the form of any observed association is almost always asymmetrical (one way). Figure 5 is a typical instance of asymmetrical association from which one observes that in the lower range of the

Table 1. Scattergram Analysis of the Association between Whig or Democratic Losses to Free Soil, 1844–48, and the Listed 1850 Census Indicators, Latitude, and Population Growth Rate of the 1840s

Indicators from, or calculated from, the 1850 United States Census and latitude	Proportional Whig Decline, 1844-48							
	Ohio			Ohio without Western Reserve		Indiana		
	nine-cell	four-cell median	four-cell mid-range	four-cell median	four-cell mid-range	nine-cell	four-cell median	four-cell mid-range
% population foreign-born	0.00	-0.27	-0.36	-0.02	+0.15	-0.20	-0.36	+0.39
% of adults in manufacturing	+0.24	+0.65	-0.26	+0.33	-0.14	-0.29	-0.36	-0.33
latitude of the county	+0.36	+0.47	+0.79	+0.01	+0.24	+0.48	+0.68	+0.81
population increase measure	-0.04	-0.27	-0.68	-0.26	+0.03	+0.23	+0.44	+0.62
farm population as a % of total population	+0.16	+0.04	+0.30	+0.09	-0.18	-0.03	-0.10	-0.30
value of farmland	+0.26	+0.53	-0.43	+0.56	+0.36	-0.10	-0.04	-0.18
% of county area in farms	+0.18	-0.05	+1.00	+0.09	+0.35	-0.26	-0.10	-0.82
% of county area in improved farmland	+0.29	-0.04	+1.00	+0.09	+0.14	-0.25	-0.36	-0.44
value of farm output per farm capita	+0.04	+0.05	-0.03	+0.33	+0.13	+0.03	-0.30	+0.48
value of farm output per improved acre	+0.33	+0.33	-0.01	+0.33	+0.61	-0.30	-0.48	-0.68
improved farmland as a % of all farmland	+0.41	+0.11	+1.00	+0.01	-0.01	-0.07	-0.17	-0.15
production of all grain per farm capita	-0.38	-0.33	-0.62	-0.09	-0.41	-0.07	-0.07	+0.13
number of all livestock per farm capita	+0.37	+0.58	+0.23	+0.74	+0.62	-0.24	-0.03	-0.28
composite agricultural[a] prosperity index	+0.04	+0.11	-0.19	+0.56	+0.30	-0.11	-0.23	-0.42

[a]This composite index is a weighted average of seven of the preceding eight indicators, excluding value of farm output per improved acre. Each indicator value is expressed as a percentage of its mean for each state or portion of a state, and the composite consists of an average of four components: value of farmland; value of farm output per farm capita; average of all grain and number of livestock per farm capita; and average of the remaining three indicators, all of which relate to stage of land usage. Using all eight indicators, weighted equally or grouped, yields almost identical composite values to the ones used here for every state or portion of a state.

Table 1 (*continued*)

	Proportional Whig Decline, 1844-48						Proportional Democratic Decline, 1844-48					
	Northern Illinois			Michigan			Pennsylvania			Illinois		
	nine-cell	four-cell		nine-cell	four-cell		nine-cell	four-cell		nine-cell	four-cell	
		median	mid-range		median	mid-range		median	mid-range		median	mid-range
	+0.62	+0.42	+0.19	-0.58	-0.76	-0.54	+0.08	+0.36	+0.06	+0.51	+0.79	+0.86
	-0.41	-0.01	-1.00	-0.23	-0.08	-0.21	+0.01	+0.23	-1.00	-0.29	-0.07	+0.35
	+0.81	+0.82	+1.00	+0.07	+0.45	+0.20	+0.45	+0.79	+0.60	+0.45	+0.87	+1.00
	+0.69	+0.58	+1.00	+0.52	+0.69	+0.73	+0.43	+0.67	+0.51	+0.59	+0.78	+1.00
	+0.09	-0.15	-0.04	+0.48	+0.57	+0.69	-0.10	-0.08	+0.39	-0.25	-0.13	-0.56
	-0.06	+0.27	-0.53	-0.48	-0.68	-1.00	-0.09	-0.36	-1.00	-0.11	-0.38	+0.30
	+0.36	+0.14	+0.42	-0.26	-0.67	-0.69	-0.35	-0.79	-0.60	-0.10	-0.25	+0.56
	+0.36	+0.55	+0.42	-0.33	-0.67	-0.69	-0.44	-0.60	-1.00	-0.07	-0.13	+0.62
	+0.06	-0.05	-0.43	-0.51	-0.64	-0.52	-0.26	-0.70	-1.00	-0.03	-0.26	+0.08
	-0.42	-0.50	-0.83	-0.40	-0.28	-0.42	0.00	+0.36	-0.11	-0.29	-0.19	-0.67
	+0.16	+0.23	-0.11	-0.43	-0.46	-0.57	-0.33	-0.70	-1.00	+0.15	+0.13	+0.28
	-0.24	-0.04	-1.00	-0.33	-0.46	-0.71	-0.17	-0.60	-0.11	-0.23	-0.43	-0.65
	-0.48	-0.42	-0.73	-0.52	-0.67	-0.55	-0.19	-0.60	-0.54	-0.44	-0.67	-0.69
	+0.10	-0.05	-0.43	-0.37	-0.67	-0.66	-0.35	-0.60	-0.25	-0.07	-0.41	-0.21

The values in the table are gammas calculated from contingency tables produced by recoding the interval values into thirds or into dichotomies divided at either medians or midranges.

Figure 5. Northern Illinois: Estimates of Whig Party Proportional Loss to the Free Soil Party in 1848 by County Plotted against Value of All Farm Output per Improved Acre in 1850

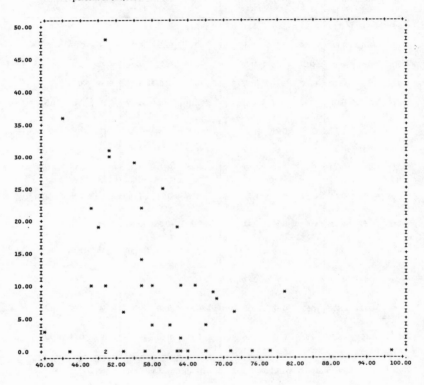

X axis = value of all farm production
Y axis = Whig party proportional loss
N = 41 (all northern Illinois counties with at least 0.5 percent Free Soil vote in 1848 that were not affected by creation of counties from 1844 through the 1850 census year)
Northern Illinois defined as counties with geographic center at or north of 40° north latitude
Value of all farm production shown as dollar value per square mile of improved farmland as a percent of $10,000

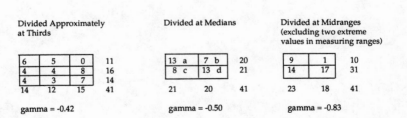

Divided Approximately at Thirds			
6	5	0	11
4	4	8	16
4	3	7	14
14	12	15	41

gamma = -0.42

Divided at Medians		
13 a	7 b	20
8 c	13 d	21
21	20	41

gamma = -0.50

Divided at Midranges (excluding two extreme values in measuring ranges)		
9	1	10
14	17	31
23	18	41

gamma = -0.83

regressor the political variable stretches over the entire range, whereas in the higher range of the regressor only low Free Soil acquisitions appear. Generally the asymmetrical associations are negative, as in this example, but occasionally they are positive, as in Figure 6. This latter instance has to be read that in the high range of the regressor (latitude), the drawing power of Free Soil spread over the range, but in the low range of the regressor, its appeal was almost always low.

An illustrative example of asymmetrical association, related in a very general way to the voter response under study here, may be found in Harold D. Bloom and H. Douglas Price's article "Voter Response to Short-Run Economic Conditions: The Asymmetric Effect of Prosperity and Recession." They report that decline in per capita income in the year preceding a congressional election disadvantaged the party holding the presidency but that rising income had no significant effect on the party's share of the vote. This is, in a sense, a one-way association: economic decline did affect some voters; economic prosperity had no such effect.[17] If the party holding the presidency had been found to gain an advantage from prosperity but suffered a loss from economic decline, this would have been a two-way association, possibly even a linear association.

There is no way to use a summary statistic such as the product-moment correlation coefficient to summarize most asymmetrical associations. A very few cases located as outliers can tilt the regression line seriously and yield either a stronger or a weaker association than would appear from nonlinear analysis. The strength of association based on a linear regression, therefore, may bear little relationship to the usefulness of inferences to be drawn from the configuration. Curvilinear relationships may be suggested by Figures 5 and 6, but obtaining a higher correlation coefficient by fitting the appropriate curve would not reveal the asymmetry in the most forthright manner. Ordered categories from which Goodman and Kruskal's gamma may be computed are a good way to observe and measure asymmetrical associations, for gamma is especially sensitive to such one-way forms of association.[18] Applied to four-cell tables, gamma is usually designated Yule's Q. With the cells lettered in the customary manner (shown on Figure 5) as $a, b, c,$ and $d, Q = ad - bc/ad + bc$. If any cell value is zero, gamma is the maximum, 1.00. Hence if one category has no predictive power but the other category is

Figure 6. Northern Illinois: Estimates of Whig Party Proportional
Loss to the Free Soil Party in 1848 by County Plotted against County
Latitude

X axis = latitude to nearest tenth (shown before the decimal point)
Y axis = Whig party proportional loss
N = 41 (all northern Illinois counties with at least 0.5 percent Free Soil vote in 1848 that were not
     affected by creation of counties from 1844 through the 1850 census year)
Northern Illinois defined as counties with geographic center at or north of 40° north latitude

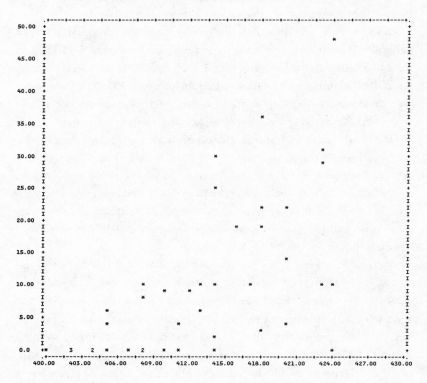

Divided Approximately at Thirds			
0	3	8	11
4	8	4	16
10	3	1	14
14	14	13	41

gamma = +0.81

Divided at Medians		
4	16	20
15	6	21
19	22	41

gamma = +0.82

Divided at Midranges (excluding one extreme value in measuring Y range)		
0	10	10
19	12	31
19	22	41

gamma = +1.00

found entirely in one cell, this asymmetrical association is revealed in the maximizing of gamma. Kendall's *tau* is a measure of the overall association in such a table, but gamma will better reflect the majority of relationships I am using because they are usually so asymmetrical.

A straightforward discussion of the underlying models of many summary statistics for contingency tables may be found in Herbert F. Weisberg's "Models of Statistical Relationship." Referring to Yule's Q as used in summarizing cross-tabulations of legislative votes by party, Weisberg comments that though "this model regards statistical independence as the null value condition," Q accepts "a single cohesive party as the definition of a perfect relationship." This is an example of asymmetry in which belonging to one party predicts a vote perfectly though belonging to the other party does not.[19] Illustrations of gamma and Q values to summarize a scattergram with values recoded to collapse into nine-cell or four-cell contingency tables appear below in further discussion of Figures 5 and 6.

Including ninety-six other scattergrams at this point in the chapter is hardly a viable option. Hence, even though I know of no entirely satisfactory way of conveying the implications of each relationship through use of summary statistics, gamma values from nine-cell tables and from four-cell tables will have to serve the purpose. The nine-cell cross-tabulations involve collapsing values into approximate thirds of the cases for each attribute. Two different four-cell cross-tabulations are provided, one using the medians and the other using the midranges (with evident extreme values excluded from measurement of ranges though not from the contingency tables).[20] The distribution of values in some of the variables is so bad, however, that even gamma can be misleading. Figures 5 and 6 offer an opportunity to observe the differing clues each of these gamma values provides for attempting to envision the scattergram and assess its implications.

Figure 5 shows the forty-one usable counties of northern Illinois with Whig proportional loss plotted against value of all farm output per improved acre. Collapsing these values into nine cells permits considerable impact on gamma's value from slender value differences in both variables and yields a gamma value of -0.42. In both the low and middle columns for farm production the Whig loss is well distributed among the three rows, with a slight preponderance in the high row. In the high farm production column, however, Whig loss is located entirely in the low and middle rows with none in the high row. Collapsing values into only four cells, divided at the medians, reveals that counties below the median in farm production were more likely to have high Whig losses to Free Soil, whereas counties above the median in farm production were almost twice as likely to be in the low Whig-loss row. The gamma value is −0.50. Four cells using the midranges offer a clearer impression of the more extreme values, by leaving the large proportion of cases with narrow distinctions in values compressed into two cells, and most fully reveal the extent of the asymmetrical relationship: counties below the midrange in farm production are in both low and high Whig-loss rows, but counties above the midrange in farm production are, with only one exception, below midrange in Whig loss. Even though a contingency table should be analyzed as in the preceding comment from the side of the presumed independent variable (farm production), asking where the above-midrange Whig loss occurred reinforces the image of asymmetrical association: nine of those ten counties are in the low farm production column; in other words, Whig losses to Free Soil were above midrange almost exclusively in the less prosperous agricultural areas. The gamma value of −0.83 reflects this almost maximum asymmetrical association.

Figure 6 provides the plot of Whig losses against latitude of each county. Such a clear positive asymmetrical association is shown that each way of cross-tabulating and obtaining gamma values points strongly to the form of the association. The southern part of northern Illinois had only low Whig losses, but in the northern part losses were scattered throughout the range. The nine-cell cross-tabulation shows that in the column for the southernmost third of northern Illinois (lower third of latitude values) Whig losses were preponderantly low and none was high. The column for the thirteen northernmost counties shows a strikingly reverse distribution. The +0.81 gamma value measures the extremity of this association. Using medians for four cells shows fifteen of nineteen more southerly counties below median in Whig losses and also points toward a two-way association because northernmost counties preponderantly were above the median in Whig losses. The analysis giving greater weight to extreme values in the skewed distribution of the Whig losses is the midrange division into four cells. Here the twenty-two counties north of midrange are nearly equally divided between those above and below midrange in Whig losses, but all nineteen of the counties south of midrange are below midrange in Whig losses. The empty cell a yields a $+1.00$ gamma value, illustrating the maximizing of gamma where one category (south of midrange latitude) is a perfect predictor of the political category even though the other category (north of midrange latitude) is of little use in predicting the political category.

Table 1 provides the three gamma values for the forms of contingency tables discussed above for each of the ninety-eight scattergrams. The fourteen regressor variables are arranged in the following order: percentage of population foreign-born; percentage of adults in manufacturing; latitude; two measures that may suggest that a county is underdeveloped, rapid population growth and farmers as a proportion of total population; eight possible indexes of agricultural prosperity; and a very general composite agricultural prosperity index that is the average of seven of the eight separate indexes of prosperity weighted to obtain approximately equal weight for each. For each of the states or portions of states used for Table 1, these seven measures (excluding value of farm production per improved acre) are positively and usually strongly intercorrelated—and negatively correlated with each of the indexes of underdevelopment. For each state or portion of a state used, the composite index of farm prosperity correlates positively and usually very strongly with every one of the eight separate indexes of prosperity and negatively with both indexes of underdevelopment. With much humility in seeking to characterize so complex a matter as rural and village economic patterns from county-aggregate indicators, I think the prosperity indexes suggest a mature and prospering agricultural society. On the other hand, proportion of county population in farming above midrange probably suggests frontier regions; and counties growing exceptionally rapidly probably were less developed unless urban growth was involved.

In Table 1 there is no consistent relationship between the foreign-born proportion of the population and Free Soil losses. The same is evident for proportion of adults in manufacturing. As mentioned previously, neither one provides unambiguous clues or helps with any general assessment of the response of nativists or workers to Free Soil.

Latitude and the agricultural prosperity measures do generally appear to be associated with Whig losses in Indiana, northern Illinois, and Michigan—as well as with Democratic losses in Pennsylvania and all of Illinois. Ohio is exceptional enough to require separate comment. That Free Soil was a symbolic issue for antislavery sentiment is supported by the positive associations between latitude and major party losses. That Free Soil was a self-interest issue is supported by the evidence that in each area except Ohio where farm prosperity prevailed, the appeal of Free Soil was blunted, whereas in newer and developing areas, the appeal of Free Soil was unpredictable, ranging from low to high. The inference would be that satisfactory agricultural conditions produced few self-interest concerns about keeping the westward lands free from slavery, but that less satisfactory agricultural conditions led some to eye the frontier and have a personal interest in Free Soil.

Ohio does not follow this pattern. Detailed examination revealed that the counties where Whig loss to Free Soil was the highest were in the Western Reserve of northeastern Ohio, where men such as Congressman Joshua R. Giddings had long led antislavery forces. The highest Whig losses occurred in the four counties in Giddings's district and four of the five contiguous counties, and the other contiguous county was not far behind.[21] Obviously, Free Soil as a symbolic issue dominated self-interest here. Removing these counties and recalculating for the remainder of Ohio only strengthens the evidence that the reverse of expectation was the case in Ohio: in areas of prosperous agriculture, there was a wide range of losses to Free Soil and in less prosperous areas losses were small. I have no hypothesis to account for Ohio's exceptionalism beyond noting that the 1848 elections in Ohio were devastating to the existing party system there, cross-pressured great numbers of voters, and led to an unusually large decline in turnout. Stephen E. Maizlish in his book *The Triumph of Sectionalism: The Transformation of Ohio Politics, 1844–1856* entitles the chapter on this election "The Revolution of 1848 and the Roots of the New Alignment."[22] Probably the political maelstrom in Ohio hopelessly obscured any evidence of the self-interest dimension sought in this analysis.

Inferences about political behavior are troublesome at best. Moreover, Free Soil gains in 1848 over Liberty party support in 1844 were generally slight and did not vary much among most counties. This means that the dependent variables are too poorly distributed and too skewed toward low values to serve well in regression analysis. Scattergram inspection and gamma values from ordered categories, nonetheless, in my judgment, suggest that the leading issue of Free Soil does appear to have strengthened antislavery with a self-interest appeal to voters concerned with the territories, either for themselves or for their children. The symbolic appeal of Free Soil as merely another way of attacking slavery cannot be measured directly from an association study such as I have been doing, but it can be inferred from the pervasive and positive relation between latitude and Free Soil appeal. If, as much persuasive evidence indicates, closeness to slave regions muted hostility somewhat and distance facilitated a stereotyped image of the enemy, the prominence of latitude in predicting the success of Free Soil in wooing former Whigs and Democrats suggests a strong component of generalized antislavery sentiment in the votes of those drawn to the Free Soil banner for the first time in 1848. A word of caution about Pennsylvania is in order, however, because many of the defecting Democrats were in poorer counties near the New York border. It may be impossible to separate Van Buren factionalism from self-interest or symbolic antislavery in Free Soil appeal there.

Town workers are not distinguishable in these data, but what little evidence there may be lies in the proportion of a county's adult population employed in manufacturing jobs and would have to be drawn from Pennsylvania. In that state the Free Soil appeal was most likely to be strong in areas where very few were employed in manufacturing, though the midrange gamma value on Table 1 results from only the six counties of greatest Democratic loss, all of which were below midrange in proportion of adults employed in manufacturing. Even in Ohio so few counties reported substantial employment in manufacturing that the variance for this attribute measure is not adequate for analysis by scattergram or contingency table. The mean for Ohio counties is less than 4 percent with a small standard deviation of 3.5 percent. West of Ohio the proportions of adults employed in manufacturing were even smaller. The mean for Illinois counties, for example, was 1.8 percent with a standard deviation of not even 2 percent. A recent study of signatures on antislavery petitions suggests that a significant proportion were those of town workers in shops or factories. The design of my investigation does not permit a test of whether such workers were keenly antislavery or the evaluation of any other assessment of the "Free Labor" aspect of the Free Soil appeal in 1848.[23]

Before concluding my appraisal of the Free Soil party of 1848 as a harbinger of the breakup of the existing party system, I need to raise our sights once more to regression estimates of continuity and shifting among voters between 1848 and 1860. This is a very limited endeavor, simply addressing the question of how important the defections from a party in 1848 proved to be to the emergence of a new two-party system in the North. Unless one denies the strong affective attachment to party among the mass of voters, as I do not, the logistics of creating a decisively winning combination among the anti-Democrats had to culminate in drawing a significant number of former Democrats into the opposition. I do not question that this task was infinitely complicated, or that the nativist movement of the period played an important and often inconsistent role, but I cannot escape the conclusion that such ultimate success throughout the North as the Republican party achieved in 1860 depended on attracting significant numbers of former Democrats, whatever the lure or avenue of crossing over.

Whether mobilizing new voters was a crucial element in gains for the Republican party is difficult to know with certainty. If greatly increased turnout disproportionately advantaged Republicans, the Democratic share of the total vote could have declined without substantial Democratic defection to the Republicans. This, in turn, should be reflected in a positive association between increased turnout and Democratic losses in share of total vote between 1852 and 1856. For the counties of the North excluding New York State, this rarely happened. There was a decisive increase in turnout in the great majority of counties, but Democratic losses were meaningfully associated with the increases for only a few counties. In Pennsylvania counties with greatest Democratic loss turnout was only slightly increased. There is no association between county-level change in turnout and Democratic loss in Ohio, Illinois, or Michigan. Of Indiana's eighty-seven usable counties, only seven in which turnout was greatly increased had higher Democratic losses.

To place the Free Soil role in this shifting process in some perspective, the element of continuity in Democratic voting by county is useful.[24] New York was unique and must be excluded in any effort to assess the

degree of continuity in Democratic voting, and that state is excluded
from the following analysis. In New York there were third-party surges
in both 1848 and 1856 (with New Yorkers as third-party candidates in
both years) that would distort the regression analysis of continuity in the
North elsewhere. In addition, the unique circumstance in Pennsylvania
in 1860 that led to a desperate Democratic fusion effort on the southern
Democrat (John C. Breckinridge) electors and drove hoards of Democrats into not voting, further distorts the trend with this short-term
deviation, and Pennsylvania counties are excluded from regressions
involving 1860.

Democratic party county-aggregate continuity from 1840 to 1844 has
already been offered as an example of maximum expected continuity
(Figure 1), with a weighted regression yielding a standard error of
estimate of 3.26 percent and an estimate of Democratic gain throughout the North of approximately 1 percent of the total vote.[25] From 1844
to 1848 the weighted regression ($r = .86$) provides a standard error of
estimate of 6 percent, reflecting the disturbance among Democratic
voters in several states other than New York, especially in Pennsylvania
and Illinois. The Democrats' estimated net loss is, however, only 4.61
percent of the total northern vote (outside New York). Table 2 furnishes
the statistics from pairwise comparisons of the Democratic percentage
of total vote in successive pairs of elections. The weighted regression for
1848 to 1852 indicates an almost identical strength of association as for
the 1844–48 quadrennium ($r = .88$; standard error of estimate $= 4.86$
percent) and yields an estimate of Democratic net gain of 3.18 percent
of the total vote of the North, substantially canceling out the Democratic
losses to Free Soil in 1848 outside New York. Although the Free Soil
leadership was encouraged by getting more votes than the Liberty party
had eight years earlier, the Free Soil party experienced substantial declines almost everywhere in the North between 1848 and 1852. North-
wide, Free Soil lost 30 percent of its 1848 share of total vote, down from
10.9 percent of the total vote in 1848 to 7.65 percent in 1852.[26]

It was during the succeeding four years, when the Kansas-Nebraska
Act evidently galvanized antislavery leadership and nativism surfaced
dramatically, that the Democrats lost their largest component to the
opposition. The 1852–56 weighted regression yields an estimate of
5.27 percent net loss for the Democrats—more than their estimated

Table 2. Weighted Regressions for Democratic Party Percentage of Total Presidential Vote of Counties of the North[a]

	1840-44[b]	1844-48	1848-52	1852-56	1856-60[c]
r	0.93	0.86	0.88	0.80	0.94
R^2	0.86	0.74	0.78	0.64	0.88
a	6.45	-6.81	14.50	-4.08	4.41
b	0.89	1.04	0.77	0.98	0.89
Std. error of estimate	3.26	6.00	4.86	7.47	4.23
Least-squares estimate of continuity	95.8%	97.6%	91.9%	93.54%	93.4%
Unweighted N[d]	433	411	468	519	505
Net gain or loss as a percentage of the Democratic party share:					
	+2.28	-9.22	+6.36	-10.54	-2.16
Net gain or loss as a percentage of the total vote of the North:					
	+1.14	-4.61	+3.18	-5.27	-1.08
From northwide aggregate returns: Democratic % of total vote					
1st Election	47.17%	48.73%	44.06%	49.16%	41.61%
2nd Election	48.77%	44.06%	49.16%	43.34%	42.65%
	(48.73%)[e]			(41.61%)[f]	
Absolute % change	+1.60	-4.67	+5.10	-5.82	+1.04

[a]Weighting is by total vote in the first of each pair of elections. The counties of New York State are excluded from all except the 1840-44 regression; also the counties of Pennsylvania are excluded from the 1856-60 regression.

[b]These weighted values differ from the unweighted values shown in Figure 1 and discussed previously.

[c]For 1860 the Democratic party percentage of the total vote is the combined percentages for the Stephen A. Douglas and the John C. Breckinridge electors.

[d]Except for exclusion of New York State and Pennsylvania as indicated in note a, all counties of the North are used except those involved in boundary changes because of the creation of new counties in any of the five years spanning the pair of elections.

[e]Excluding the counties of New York State.

[f]Excluding the counties of Pennsylvania and New York State.

loss to Free Soil in 1848. And there the losses almost ended, for between 1856 and 1860 the Democrats behaved very consistently in the county-aggregate proportions of total vote ($r = .94$; standard error of estimate = 4.23 percent) and lost only 1 additional percent of the northern vote, outside New York and Pennsylvania.

Given the losses in 1844–48, the recovery in 1848–52, the larger losses in 1852–56, and the near stability in 1856–60, between 1848 and 1860 the northern Democrats suffered a net defection, and the largest single loss may be traced to the quadrennium in which the Kansas-Nebraska Act and aroused nativism disturbed northern political waters deeply. Scattergrams for the succession of Democratic county-aggregate proportions of total vote visually illustrate the degree of ecological continuity, which I find impressive in light of the many sources of disturbance mentioned at the beginning of this chapter. The unweighted regression values from the scattergrams are close to the weighted values in Table 2, though the weighted associations are usually stronger. And the strength of association between Democratic losses in the 1844–48 period and Democratic gains in the succeeding four-year interval is at least suggestive ($r = .75$; $a = 0$; $b = 1.35$) though the standard error of estimate is large at 16 percent partly because of some extreme outliers that represent counties where Democrats made spectacular gains. The succeeding Democratic losses between 1852 and 1856 are so modestly correlated with their gains from 1848 to 1852, despite the positive association evident in the scattergram, that it appears that many new sources of Democratic defections entered the arena ($r = .46$).

The Kansas-Nebraska Act was generally considered a major source of alarm among those concerned with keeping the territories free of slavery. It also serves as a centerpiece in the generalized perception throughout the North of a Slave Power conspiracy, so that it may have served as both a self-interest issue to prospective migrants and a more symbolic antislavery focus for condemnation of the entire slave establishment. Plotting the percentage decline in Democratic share of total vote between 1852 and 1856 against the census indicators employed for study of the earlier Free Soil defections of 1848 provides some evidence. Population growth during the 1850s here replaces growth during the 1840s.

The gamma values for the three forms of cross-tabulation used for

Table 3. Scattergram Analysis of the Associations between Democratic Losses to Opposition Parties, 1852–56, and the Listed 1850 Census Indicators, Latitude, and Population Growth Rate of the 1850s

Indicators from, or calculated from, the 1850 United States Census and latitude	Pennsylvania			Ohio			Northern Ohio	
	nine-cell	four-cell median	mid-range	nine-cell	four-cell median	mid-range	four-cell median	mid-range
% population foreign-born	+0.33	+0.48	-0.37	+0.31	+0.07	+0.31	+0.17	-1.00
% of adults in manufacturing	-0.34	-0.41	-1.00	-0.27	-0.23	-0.59	-0.05	-0.63
latitude of the county	+0.72	+0.89	+0.90	+0.78	+0.91	+0.83	+0.68	+0.70
population increase measure	+0.27	+0.48	+0.53	+0.12	+0.18	+0.69	+0.35	+0.66
farm population as a % of total population	+0.58	+0.54	+0.87	+0.25	+0.37	-0.01	-0.31	-0.38
value of farmland	-0.65	-0.83	-1.00	-0.35	-0.28	-0.63	-0.21	-0.46
% of county area in farms	-0.38	-0.54	-0.18	-0.21	-0.13	-0.63	-0.35	-0.67
% of county area in improved farmland	-0.65	-0.65	-1.00	-0.16	-0.18	-0.49	-0.35	-0.61
value of farm output per farm capita	-0.45	-0.79	-0.36	-0.38	-0.46	-0.48	-0.02	-0.18
value of farm output per improved acre	-0.12	-0.20	+0.45	-0.07	+0.13	+0.01	+0.29	+0.40
improved farmland as a % of all farmland	-0.67	-0.80	-1.00	+0.01	-0.18	-0.33	-0.29	-0.54
production of all grain per farm capita	-0.64	-0.71	-1.00	-0.49	-0.60	-1.00	-0.23	-0.36
number of all livestock per farm capita	+0.32	+0.27	-0.20	-0.09	+0.03	-0.32	+0.08	+0.09
composite agricultural[a] prosperity index	-0.65	-0.76	-1.00	-0.36	-0.28	-0.50	-0.36	-0.21

[a]See note a on Table 1.

1848 are given in Table 3. Latitude proved to be so decisive in Ohio, Indiana, and Illinois, with a large proportion of counties in the southern areas having had no Democratic losses, that plotting was done for the northern parts of these states and gamma values calculated using the medians and midranges of the northern counties of these three states. The foreign-born proportion again provides ambiguous signals, but this time more evidence emerges that nativist reaction to foreign-born concentrations may have helped the Republicans. The proportion of

Table 3 (*continued*)

Indiana			Northern Indiana		Illinois			Northern Illinois		Michigan		
nine-cell	four-cell median	mid-range	four-cell median	mid-range	nine-cell	four-cell median	mid-range	four-cell median	mid-range	nine-cell	four-cell median	mid-range
0.00	+0.19	+0.34	+0.05	-0.13	+0.59	+0.65	+0.91	+0.56	+0.38	-0.22	-0.01	-1.00
+0.01	+0.21	+0.41	+0.15	-0.48	-0.08	-0.25	+0.02	-0.25	-0.20	0.00	-0.29	-1.00
+0.75	+0.72	+0.83	+0.25	+0.16	+0.65	+0.78	+0.76	+0.78	+0.96	-0.04	-0.01	-0.33
+0.28	+0.09	+0.29	+0.33	-0.20	+0.60	+0.57	+0.23	+0.34	+0.10	+0.12	+0.29	+0.25
-0.06	-0.36	+0.04	-0.42	-0.36	+0.09	+0.17	-0.06	+0.25	-0.03	-0.33	+0.27	-0.05
+0.13	+0.28	+0.03	+0.04	+0.08	+0.31	+0.45	+0.51	-0.21	-0.20	-0.15	+0.11	-0.05
-0.28	-0.14	+0.03	-0.05	-0.16	+0.04	-0.26	+0.71	-0.17	+0.57	-0.30	-0.29	-0.34
-0.30	+0.09	-0.22	-0.24	-0.08	+0.10	-0.05	+0.58	0.00	+0.36	-0.23	-0.29	-0.65
+0.05	+0.12	+0.36	+0.24	+0.18	+0.13	+0.30	-0.02	-0.42	-1.00	-0.11	-0.17	-0.43
-0.09	-0.14	-0.32	-0.33	-0.21	-0.42	-0.49	-0.42	-0.73	-0.74	+0.16	-0.01	+0.29
-0.08	+0.14	+0.10	+0.15	+0.36	+0.22	+0.42	+0.46	-0.33	+0.10	+0.09	-0.29	-0.10
-0.32	-0.28	-0.14	-0.24	+0.02	+0.06	+0.17	-0.63	-0.56	-1.00	+0.15	+0.27	+0.14
-0.49	-0.52	-0.60	-0.24	+0.41	-0.47	-0.39	-0.73	-0.41	-0.51	-0.09	-0.01	-0.36
-0.06	-0.03	-0.28	-0.05	+0.10	+0.19	+0.35	-0.08	-0.51	-0.48	-0.06	-0.35	-0.42

The values in the table are gammas calculated from contingency tables produced by recoding the interval values into thirds or into dichotomies divided at either medians or midranges.

adults in manufacturing is even more negatively associated with Democratic losses than with Whig or Democratic losses in 1848 but is based on such a limited range of values that any inferences should be very guarded.

The importance of latitude except for Michigan reinforces the symbolic interpretation of all sectional issues in the 1856 election. This consistently positive asymmetrical association between latitude and the tendency in 1856 toward Democratic desertion to the opposition is far clearer than for Democratic and Whig defections in 1848. For the forty-six usable counties of northern Illinois (north of latitude 39.9) the relationship is unusually linear, with an r value of +0.74. Again, this may be employed to infer that distance from slave territory facilitated a symbolic negative-reference-group perception among northerners apart from self-interest concern with the danger that slavery would get a foothold in the territories.

What of the agricultural prosperity indicators? The negative association of prosperity with Democratic loss is not the same as for 1848, but it is clearly present. For Indiana associations are weaker, but this time Ohio falls into line.[27] And though for all Illinois the indications are mixed, for northern Illinois they are strongly in the expected pattern. The self-interest appeal of free soil in its 1856 form was generally stronger for many in less prosperous agricultural areas but for far fewer in the prosperous ones.

Was the Free Soil party of 1848, then, the harbinger of the disruption of the two-party system? Of course, in some ways, it was. Getting the first olive out of the bottle is an achievement not to be dismissed lightly, and having a former Democratic president as the presidential candidate must have given comfort to Democrats everywhere who had an inclination to bolt. Yet apparently most bolters came home swiftly. Having defected once, they were presumably more susceptible to renewed free-soil appeals. Comparing the Democratic percentage loss to the Free Soil party in 1848 with the Democratic percentage loss eight years later in 1856 by scattergram analysis suggests that much of the defection did occur in the same counties as in 1848, but the strength of association is not good ($r = .61$; $a = 6$; $b = .67$; standard error of estimate = 12 percent). Moreover, a fifth of the counties of the North showed Democratic losses in 1856 but none in 1848. The continuing impact of the earlier experience need not be entirely dismissed to view the 1856 shifts, larger than in any previous interval between presidential elections, as having an additional and separate impetus. The free-soil appeal had been given a decade of intense public exposure by 1856, and many voters already sensitized to both its self-interest and its symbolic appeal probably considered it far more relevant when prospective regions of settlement not far to the west were stripped of the generation-old free-soil guarantee provided in the Missouri Compromise than when the target territory had been faraway New Mexico, Utah, and Oregon.

In my judgment, there is strong evidence to assign the 1848 episode a significant supporting role in the analysis of the disruption of the second party system but to continue to look to the Kansas-Nebraska controversy and the flaring of nativism as more crucial even in bringing free soil to a new level of intensity as both a self-interest issue and a symbol for generalized antislavery perception of a Slave Power threat to enslave free men everywhere. The antislavery leaders who decided in 1848 to hitch their wagon to free-soil principles, without knowing what would transpire between 1854 and 1856, very probably advanced their ultimate cause more effectively than had they opted for a purer antislavery posture in that election.

ACKNOWLEDGMENTS

I am indebted to the following for painstakingly studying versions of this essay and offering many helpful suggestions: Lloyd E. Ambrosius in his role as editor of this volume, Thad A. Brown and the students in his seminar in voting behavior, William E. Gienapp, Donald O. Granberg, Michael F. Holt, and James L. Huston.

NOTES

1. A survey of the voluminous literature on antislavery, even in its political manifestations, seems inappropriate here. Three books bear directly, at least in part, on the subject I am examining: Frederick J. Blue, *The Free Soilers: Third Party Politics, 1848–1854* (Urbana: University of Illinois Press, 1973); Joseph G. Rayback, *Free Soil: The Election of 1848* (Lexington: University Press of Kentucky, 1970); and Richard H. Sewell, *Ballots for Freedom: Antislavery Politics in the United States, 1837–1860* (New York: Oxford University Press, 1976). Arthur M. Schlesinger, Jr., ed., *History of American Presidential Elections, 1789–1968,* 4 vols. (New York: Chelsea House, 1971), and his *History of U.S. Political Parties,* 4 vols. (New York: Chelsea House, 1973), include several relevant essays: Holman Hamilton's on the election of 1848, Roy and Jeanette Nichols's on the election of 1852,

Roy F. Nichols and Philip S. Klein's on the election of 1856, Aileen S. Kraditor's on the Liberty and Free Soil parties, and Michael F. Holt's on the Anti-Masonic and Know-Nothing parties. Michael F. Holt, *The Political Crisis of the 1850s* (New York: Wiley, 1978), provides a valuable frame of reference for every aspect of this chapter. Several state studies have considerable relevance, but none explore the ecological aspects of the Free Soil appeal to the rank and file of voters. Valuable examples include Dale Baum, *The Civil War Party System: The Case of Massachusetts, 1848–1876* (Chapel Hill: University of North Carolina Press, 1984); Ronald P. Formisano, *The Birth of Mass Political Parties: Michigan, 1827–1861* (Princeton: Princeton University Press, 1971); and Stephen E. Maizlish, *The Triumph of Sectionalism: The Transformation of Ohio Politics, 1844–1856* (Kent, Ohio: Kent State University Press, 1983). An extremely important study highly relevant to this subject is William E. Gienapp, *The Origins of the Republican Party, 1852–1856* (New York: Oxford University Press, 1987).

2. Aileen S. Kraditor, "The Liberty and Free Soil Parties," in Schlesinger, ed., *History of U.S. Political Parties*, 1: 876, 878.

3. I am using my own machine-readable data set containing county-aggregate election data from 1838 to 1878 and census data from 1850, 1860, and 1870. This data set is referred to in other papers I have published, and a full documentation would be too long to include. Upon request, I would be pleased to describe the set more fully and to refer specifically to other published references. See my "ExParte County Aggretates Et Cetera," *Social Science History* 11 (1987): 449–62.

4. Thomas B. Alexander, "The Dimensions of Voter Partisan Constancy in Presidential Elections from 1840 to 1860," in Stephen E. Maizlish and John J. Kushma, eds., *Essays on American Ante-Bellum Politics, 1840–1860* (Arlington: Published for the University of Texas at Arlington by Texas A & M Press, 1982), p. 86.

5. Kenneth J. Winkle presented startling evidence on this subject at the 1986 Organization of American Historians Annual Meeting in New York in a paper entitled "The Voters of Lincoln's Springfield: Politics and Community in the Antebellum Midwest." I have found much food for thought about ecological regression in his book *The Politics of Community: Migration and Politics in Antebellum Ohio* (Cambridge: Cambridge University Press, 1988), which he was gracious enough to permit me to read before its publication. Donald A. DeBats and associates have presented three highly·relevant papers on early settlements and voting patterns in Oregon (Social Science History Association, 1980; Australian and New Zealand American Studies Association, 1982; and the Wilson Center, 1984). Examination of poll books has attracted several scholars who have turned up scattered sets in several states.

6. Democrats gained 9 percent at the theoretically lowest range of their county-level strength but lost 4.5 percent (100 − 95.5) at the theoretically highest level, averaging 4.5 percent (9 − 4.5) across all counties. This is a convenient way to summarize the mean estimate of net Democratic gain or loss between two elections and need not involve any literal assumptions about hypothetical counties with zero or 100 percent Democratic vote in the first election. A similar estimate results from using the regression equation to estimate the 1844 Democratic percentage for a county near the 1840 mean Democratic vote, in this case with 50 percent Democratic share in 1840 ($a + bX$, where $X = 50$), i.e., 52.3 percent. This absolute gain over a 50 percent showing is 4.6 percent. Except for rounding errors, this would be the same as using the intercept and the least-squares estimate of continuity.

7. My concern here is that we may be misled into assuming more volatility in voter alignment than actually existed by regression statistics not adjusted for the effects discussed above. I do not know of any empirical way of making such adjustments, though for some of the questionable influences there should be ways of adjusting that meet social scientific standards.

8. Election returns referred to are from *The Tribune* [Whig] *Almanac and Political Register* (New York: H. Greeley, 1868). *The Tribune Almanac* with changing titles was published annually until late in the nineteenth century, but the 1838–54 set was bound in one of two volumes and the 1855–68 set in the second and offered for sale in 1868.

9. Angus Campbell et al., *The American Voter* (New York: Wiley, 1960), pp. 149–50, 213n. The authors report that about 20 percent of their respondents said they had changed party but that only about one-sixth of those reported reasons that would be classified as exclusively personal, representing 3 to 4 percent of the survey group.

10. For example, see Ray M. Shortridge, "The Voter Realignment in the Midwest during the 1850s," *American Politics Quarterly* 4 (1976): 193–222, and the books by Baum, Maizlish, and Gienapp cited above.

11. My data set is the source for all county-aggregate data. Walter Dean Burnham, *Presidential Ballots, 1836–1892* (Baltimore: Johns Hopkins Press, 1955), is the source for state and regional election information, though I have at places corrected Burnham's data when independent evidence indicated the need. Burnham's early work on this subject inspired an entire generation of political historians, and we are grateful to him for the readily available raw materials with which to get deeply involved quickly.

12. The absolute percentage loss for a party between elections is that party's percentage of total vote in the first election minus that party's percentage in the

second election. There were some counties in which one party's percentage in 1848 was greater than in 1844 so that the absolute percentage difference as calculated above was negative. Since the concern here is with loss, and even though gain might suggest unwelcome volatility, negative values were set equal to zero.

13. The mean county shift in popular vote, rather than statewide aggregate shift, is used here because ecological regression is useless without adequate variance among the counties. The mean and standard deviation for each state are therefore crucial.

14. A party's share of defection to Free Soil is estimated by adding the absolute percentage decline between 1844 and 1848 for the two major parties and percentaging each party's absolute decline on the sum of the two, i.e., if the Democratic absolute decline was 5 percent and the Whig was 15 percent, their respective shares would be 25 and 75 percent.

15. There are many variables in my data set that are the result of elaborate calculations based on considerable information which many research assistants and I collected over several years. The indicators per capita farm production and per improved acre farm production, as well as all indicators using farm capita, are among the original values we generated. Latitude is a measure of the degree of north latitude to the nearest one-tenth of a degree approximating the center of a county. When Ohio, Indiana, and Illinois are divided into southern and northern parts, northern is where county-center latitude values are greater than 39.9.

16. The calculation for proportional decline is a party's absolute percentage decline between 1844 and 1848, described in note 12, percentaged on that party's percentage of total vote in 1844, i.e., if Democratic percentage of total vote in 1844 was 40 percent and its absolute decline percentage between 1844 and 1848 was 10, the proportional decline would be 25 percent.

17. Harold D. Bloom and H. Douglas Price, "Voter Response to Short-Run Economic Conditions: The Asymmetric Effect of Prosperity and Recession," *American Political Science Review* 69 (1975): 1240–54.

18. Kendall's *tau* better measures the overall strength of association in a contingency table consisting of two ordered categories. But gamma yields higher values for one-way associations, which are almost always my concern in this chapter.

19. Herbert F. Weisberg, "Models of Statistical Relationship," *American Political Science Review* 68 (1974): 1638–55.

20. I have tried to divide the counties of a state or half state into three approximately equal groups for each regressor indicator, but for the political

variables I have compromised slightly between equal numbers of counties in each category and some judgmental assignment of ranges into low, medium, and high. The distributions of most of the variables used are so poor that no approach is entirely satisfactory.

21. Useful records of historical changes in congressional districts are Stanley B. Parsons, William W. Beach, and Michael J. Dubin, *United States Congressional Districts and Data, 1843–1883* (New York: Greenwood Press, 1986); and Stanley B. Parsons, William W. Beach, and Dan Hermann, *United States Congressional Districts, 1788–1841* (Westport, Conn.: Greenwood Press, 1978).

22. Maizlish wrote that the Ohio Western Reserve "contained Ohio's heaviest concentration of New Englanders, and for years was the Whigs' Ohio stronghold." He continued: "The Western Reserve went to extremes. Yankee Protestantism was concentrated there, untempered by the pragmatic necessities that faced Whigs in other sections of the state. Nevertheless, the Yankee heritage formed the soul of the Ohio Whig party, and was chiefly responsible for its tendency to 'politicize morality.'" If this is a fair assessment, there should be no surprise in failing to find clear evidence of Free Soil personal-interest politics among Whigs in Ohio in 1848; antislavery among Ohio Whigs was presumably symbolized by anything antisouthern. Maizlish noted that Ohio "Whig opposition to slavery extended to assaults on the South itself, for Southerners could not escape the taint of their immoral institution" (Maizlish, *Triumph of Sectionalism*, p. 15).

23. Edward Magdol, *The Antislavery Rank and File: A Social Profile of the Abolitionists' Constituency* (New York: Greenwood Press, 1986).

24. State or regional aggregate returns would provide information about Democratic party losses between 1852 and 1856 but would not incorporate any evidence that voters were generally loyal to party and not shifting about in a volatile manner. Since I am depending on Democratic losses by county, I need to argue that consistent county-aggregate behavior from election to election justifies my estimate of Democratic loss as resulting from defections and not from a musical-chairs scenario of shifting about among three parties.

25. If parties did not receive close to one-half the total vote, making estimates of net gain or loss would require that each party's percentage of loss or gain be applied to that party's share of total vote separately and then combined. But since Democrats and their combined opponents each commanded very nearly one-half of the total vote in the North in these elections, it appears a needless refinement of estimates to do more than consider them equal. These regression estimates have to arise from fewer than all of the counties of the North because all counties are excluded that were created in the period or that lost territory to

these. The net loss or gain estimates parallel the regional aggregate vote results, providing some evidence that the set of counties that I used is not seriously skewed from the entire universe of counties with regard to voting.

26. Excluding New York State, the Free Soil total vote in 1852 was only 24 percent below its vote in 1848, down from 171,301 to 130,632. But total vote increased almost 10 percent, leaving the Free Soil share depleted by 30 percent of its 1848 share of total vote.

27. Indiana's deviance in 1856 may have been attributable to the increased intensity of all issues symbolic of antisouthern sectionalism. Northern Indiana was late in being populated, and the range of Democratic defections in Indiana was not great in 1856. Even during the Civil War and beyond, Indiana's exceptional pro-South bent was evident. At this stage of the investigation, the guess would be that self-interest aspects of free soilism in 1856 were muted by cross-pressures from pro-South orientation.

CHAPTER TWO

★

SALMON P. CHASE AND THE

REPUBLICAN CONVENTIONS OF

1856 AND 1860:

BOLINGBROKE OR SINCERE REFORMER?

★

JOHN NIVEN

Those who are not careful students of the abolition movement and of political developments in the Midwest during the three
decades that preceded the Civil War are apt to wonder why Salmon P.
Chase, Free Soil senator from Ohio, twice Republican governor of that
important, populous state, and reelected to the United States Senate in
February 1860, was not a stronger candidate for the Republican presidential nominations in 1856 and 1860.

Chase, after all, was a founder of the Republican party. His free-soil
credentials were impeccable. While John C. Frémont, the party nomi-
nee in 1856, was trudging westward through the Gila River valley
toward California, Chase was electrifying the Free Soilers at their first
convention in Rochester, New York, with the slogan "no more slave

states and no more slave territory." William H. Seward, Chase's rival for the nomination in 1860, was promoting the candidacy of Zachary Taylor on the Whig ticket when Chase was stumping Ohio for Free Soil in 1848. Edward Bates, another Chase rival, was, likewise, well established in the Whig party leadership and was campaigning for Taylor in Missouri. An obscure congressman from Illinois, Abraham Lincoln, was adhering to Whig policy and condemning the James K. Polk administration's responsibility for the Mexican-American War even as Chase maneuvered the Democratic party in his home state to support repeal of the racially discriminating black laws.

All of Chase's rivals were antislavery men, and all eventually pledged opposition to the extension of slavery into the territories. But none could match Chase's record in this respect, nor could anyone doubt his devotion to the cause even though it was tempered by his commitment to act within what eminent jurists such as Joseph Story declared were both legal and constitutional limits. As far back as 1828, Chase, a struggling schoolteacher in Washington, had helped prepare a petition asking Congress to abolish slavery in the District of Columbia.[1] In executive and administrative experience, too, Chase was Seward's equal and far outstripped Frémont, Bates, and Lincoln. Yet Chase's party rejected him twice for nomination to the post he was not only well qualified to fill but deserved, if his contributions to the platforms and the organization of the Republican party were considered.

Some historians of the period have explained Chase's failure to secure the prize as stemming from his radicalism on the slavery issue and his posture as a sectional candidate. Others, notably Reinhard Luthin in his study of the Lincoln campaign, have pointed to Chase's failure to develop an efficient organization, particularly in the East but also in his own region, where Thurlow Weed and William H. Seward had extended their reach for delegates into Wisconsin and Michigan.

All of these explanations have a certain plausibility, but none of them goes to the root of the matter: the personality, the character, and the background of Salmon P. Chase. As a politician he was not trusted even by close associates. His family and his education marked him as an aristocrat in the frontier city where he settled. And even after Cincinnati became a more populous, cosmopolitan urban center in the 1840s and 1850s, Chase's eastern college background and his Episcopalian faith did not evoke the mass enthusiasm that would have made him more attractive to his political associates. His uncle was Ohio's first Episcopal bishop and a close friend of Henry Clay. Another uncle had served two terms as a United States senator from Vermont and had been chief justice of that state's supreme court. Other close relatives were professional men—physicians, lawyers, and clergymen—from New England's upper class. Chase's father had been a prosperous farmer, a justice of the peace, and a member for many years of the New Hampshire state senate. Chase certainly had connections, but they were not ones that aroused popular enthusiasm. And even his denomination was suspect among the Baptists, the Methodists, and later the German Protestants, who made up a majority of the voters in Ohio. Apart from his social background and his religion, his political course was extremely vulnerable to the charge of inconstancy or of opportunism in the pursuit of personal power.

Even his devotion to human rights for blacks, which he had publicly espoused since the late 1830s, when he began to defend fugitive slaves in Cincinnati, was considered circumspect by many, who claimed that these well-publicized cases were primarily self-serving. Others saw him as ingratiating himself with the rich and powerful in Ohio, the Ludlows, the McLeans, the Longworths, and the Smiths of his home city and his fellow Yankees in the prospering Western Reserve, many of whom had drifted into an antislavery, though not abolitionist, stance since the Missouri debates.[2]

Still, Chase's political career seemed most open to question. When he arrived in Cincinnati to practice law in 1830, he made no secret of his opposition to President Andrew Jackson. During the late summer of 1832, he wrote a close friend in New Haven, Connecticut, that "Jackson is plainly endeavouring to set himself above the law and the Constitution. If he should be re-elected all is lost. The west is ruined. The distress of the mercantile community is now great." For the next three years, while building up his law practice and frequenting the drawing rooms of Cincinnati's first citizens, Chase identified with the emerging Whig organization. He became a member of the Whig state committee of correspondence whose roster listed sixty-seven of the state's leading political and business figures. His marriage to Catherine Garniss, whose father was a rich Cincinnati merchant, drew Chase more deeply into the movers and shakers of the Whig party. And in an editorial for the *Cincinnati American,* he announced that he favored a protective tariff and a system of internal improvements at the federal government's expense. Although he had originally backed John McLean, he eventually supported Henry Clay for president.[3]

In 1840, Chase was still in the Whig ranks and voted for William Henry Harrison. At that time he was a Whig member of the Cincinnati city council, his first elective office. He had been quick to proclaim his antislavery views in defense of fugitive slaves and was equally quick to sense a shift in the public mood on the temperance question. But displaying a lifelong political characteristic, he moved with caution at a city council meeting during the week of March 13, 1841. With an eye on the votes of the drinking population, he did not back prohibition for Cincinnati but proposed only that no additional licenses he granted for taverns and hotels. His motion carried. "I don't know what the effect may be on me personally," said a wary Chase, "but I believe that I have done right."[4] Chase's attempt to straddle the issue backfired. He was branded a temperance man and largely on this basis was defeated for a second term on the council.

When Chase acted to restrain the spread of drinking establishments within the city limits, he had been a permanent resident of Ohio for ten years. He had seen its population almost double to make it the third most populous state in the Union. Hamilton County, in which Cincinnati was located, had enjoyed spectacular growth, far above the state average. Many of the new settlers were of foreign birth and tended to vote the Democratic ticket not only out of preference for the Democrats' presumed equal rights philosophy but, more important, because their party, with the benefit of age and experience, was much better organized than the Whig party. To an ambitious would-be politician like young Chase, these facts were far more important than any party ideology.

But he made one last effort to enter the ranks of Whig leadership. He sought the Whig nomination for state senator from Hamilton County. Local Whig politicians unanimously rejected his candidacy on the grounds that he was a radical antislavery man. After this rebuff Chase helped form the Liberty party in Ohio. He was prepared to capitalize, if at all possible, on what he perceived to be the future of political parties in his own state and, he hoped, the nation. In this respect, Chase's commitment to the moral aspects of the antislavery cause dovetailed neatly with his realistic appraisal of the position of the two parties in Ohio, and especially his home base in Cincinnati.

At this time Chase was a handsome, imposing figure, a reasonably successful lawyer who was well known to the legal fraternity throughout the state as the author of a new edition of Ohio statutes, which almost immediately became the standard work and which both Chancellor James Kent and Justice Story complimented for its accuracy and scope. He was, however, an indifferent public speaker with a decided lisp, whose arguments in court and speeches on the hustings were more impressive for their content than their dramatic presentation. Rutherford B. Hayes said that his platform style was "without much power, very pure, forcible English, but unimpassioned and spiritless."[5] Chase was obviously impressive to his contemporaries; but as an aspiring politician, he totally lacked the warmth that attracted passionate adherents. This quality was, then as now, indispensable for a successful partisan leader.

Chase's diffidence in all likelihood developed as a personality trait from the uncertainties of his childhood and adolescence in a fatherless home in which the mother struggled to maintain her large family's standing in the little New England community of Keene, New Hampshire. At an early age Chase was placed under the care of his uncle, the redoubtable Bishop Philander Chase. This experience seems to have left an indelible mark on Chase's character. At the time, Bishop Chase was seeking to further the Episcopal cause in Ohio and maintain himself and his family on a frontier farm near the village of Worthington. The bishop, a large man with piercing, nearsighted eyes that were magnified by the spectacles he habitually wore, was something of a domestic tyrant who cloaked his irascible temperament in scriptural homilies.

Young Chase had to earn his keep through never-ending farm work under the censorious eye of the bishop, who always demanded an accounting when he returned from his frequent proselytizing trips. Chase described his uncle years later, after time had mellowed his image of the bishop, as "often very harsh and severe, not because he liked to be, but because he was determined to have everything just as he thought it ought to be. . . . Certainly he lived to govern; but he liked to

govern for the good of others, not his own." A highly emotional adoles-
cent, Chase was forced to curb his temper in the presence of his imper-
ious uncle, but not before there were several clashes of will. Bishop
Chase recognized this trait, and when his nephew left his tutelage to
attend Dartmouth College, he wrote his brother Baruch that Chase's
"temper is not good, tho' much modified by discipline. His genius [is]
extraordinarily good. If he finds someone to govern and direct him
aright, he will with God's blessing make one of the first of men; if
otherwise, he may make one of the worst."[6]

One of the most important things he learned from his ordeal with the
bishop was self-control. Unfortunately, this personality trait seems to
have led to an excessive internalizing of his feelings. The bishop certainly stimulated Chase's ambition to an unusual degree through his
strict regimen and his insistence on managing not only his family but his
congregations. Chase likely emulated this trait in the older man, whom
he both admired and disliked intensely.

Chase indulged his craving for management in his organization of the
Liberty party in Ohio during 1842. From his own experience, a consum-
ing interest in the political process, and his perception that public
morals had become corrupt and decadent, Chase recognized that he
could make no headway with either of the two major parties on slavery
or any other reform issue. From his research for his edition of the *Ohio
Statutes* and in developing his arguments in the fugitive slave cases, he
had reinforced an early assumption that Congress had the constitutional power to prescribe conditions for the government of the territories. The Northwest Ordinance, in particular, had claimed his attention.
He had focused on this legislation when he wrote his brief history of
Ohio as an introduction to the *Ohio Statutes*.

Chase was, of course, familiar with the work of the New England
abolitionists and with William Lloyd Garrison's *Liberator.* He also knew
about the New York abolitionists who had broken with Garrison on the
question of political action. As a lawyer and a careful student of the
Constitution, Chase, like the New York abolitionist Gerrit Smith, could
not approve of Garrison's direct action program of combating slavery
wherever it existed. He clearly saw slavery as a local institution protected
by state legislation and community opinion. This view was not original,
nor did it break new ground in Ohio. Benjamin Wade, a state senator

during the 1837–38 sessions of the Ohio legislature, Joshua Giddings, a Whig congressman, and the Virginia-born Democrat Thomas Morris, who had served a term in the United States Senate, all held similar positions to Chase's on the exclusion of slavery from the territories.[7]

If the latent antislavery feeling that Chase believed was widespread in the North could be focused through a third party based on halting the spread of slavery in the territories, the issue could be popularized, especially in the West, where many interests were involved in the expansion of free soil. Equally important, the issue avoided any taint of illegality or opposition to constitutional guarantees on slavery. Although Chase's fellow townsman and onetime client James G. Birney had received only seven thousand votes nationwide in the 1840 presidential election as the candidate for the frankly abolitionist Liberty party, Chase was intrigued with the idea of modifying the abolitionist stigma of this party. He hoped to broaden the Liberty party's appeal beyond the antislavery movement, though that would remain primary, by having it take a stand on other political issues such as the tariff, currency, land policy, and banks. In so doing, Chase was moving away from the mainstream of abolitionist strategy.

In the late fall of 1841, Chase, on his own responsibility, drafted and put out a call for a Liberty party state convention to meet in Columbus on December 29, 1841. Birney and others in Cincinnati helped him with the mailing lists and the printing costs. Chase wrote the keynote address of the convention but did not manage to convince his associates that the party should embrace a broader platform. Some two hundred delegates from thirty-six counties met at the appointed time and approved a series of resolutions that arraigned slavery as a moral evil, asserting that it was a local, not a national, institution. Slavery should be abolished by act of Congress in the District of Columbia and in the territories or, as the resolution read, excluded "from all places within the constitutional jurisdiction of the General Government." Abolitionist delegates who clung to the Liberty party's one issue—its antislavery platform—opposed a broader series of resolutions. They were joined by others who had hitherto followed the Whig party line. Chase had included among his resolutions the hallowed Democratic positions on hard money and rigid economy in public expenditures.[8] Clearly, he wanted to offer some bait to the Democrats of his own county. His flirtation with the Whig party was now a thing of the past. Chase brushed aside complaints but saw to it that the convention nominated Leicester King for governor. King had been a well-respected Whig state senator. Chase also called for a national party convention.

In the state election, the Liberty ticket polled 5,305 votes in Ohio, not as many as Chase had hoped but enough to cause some consternation among leaders of the established parties. Chase's Democratic leanings, even if they were based on a practical assessment of the political situation in Ohio, brought stern warnings from eastern Liberty party men. After a talk with Birney, who had just returned from a trip to New York and New England, Chase felt compelled to explain his course to Gerrit Smith. Chase tried to reassure Smith that the widening of the Liberty platform would not submerge the antislavery movement in either of the two major parties.

Smith remained unconvinced. Nor was Chase able to restrain his fellow delegates at the first national convention of the Liberty party from adopting a resolution that the Fugitive Slave Law was immoral, illegal, and should not be obeyed. Chase attended this convention at Buffalo in August 1843 and wrote the platform, which marked his retreat from identifying the party with issues other than abolition or containment of slavery.[9] The Liberty party made a much more impressive showing in 1844. Birney, again its presidential candidate, received over sixty thousand votes. In New York his showing was sufficient to defeat Henry Clay and elect James K. Polk as the new Democratic president.

Events on the national scene improved the outlook for the Liberty party in states like Ohio, where the Whigs and the Democrats were evenly balanced. From 1845 through 1848, Chase maneuvered to guide the Liberty party into Democratic channels with the avowed notion that it would purify that old, established party and bring it to a free-soil position. To such Liberty party men as William Birney, James G. Birney's son and surrogate in Cincinnati, his posture smacked of opportunism. The younger Birney wrote his father just after the election of 1844 impugning Chase's free-soil principles. "In this city, we have Chase and others," he wrote, "who belong to the temporizing bargain and sale class of politicians and are frequently hazarding our cause by their recommendation of petty demagogical tricks to gain a largely increased and floating vote." In an address that Chase wrote for the Southern and

Western Liberty convention held at Cincinnati on June 11–12, 1845, he analyzed both major parties for their moral values. He found that the Democratic party had by far the soundest principles. The Whig party's "natural position," he said, "is conservative. Its natural bond of union is regard for interests rather than rights." According to Chase, both parties had antislavery elements, but both were controlled either by an oligarchy of slaveowners or by those who did their bidding. There was some hope from a revitalized Democracy but no hope from the Whigs.[10]

Chase's tilt toward the Democratic party did not go unchallenged from his Liberty party colleagues both within and outside Ohio. Gerrit Smith again attacked Chase's position, this time with a public letter reiterating the one-issue platform the party had originally adopted in 1840.[11] And, of course, the two major parties in Ohio would have nothing to do with Chase's overtures. The Mexican-American War, the Wilmot Proviso, and the rupture of the Democratic party in New York were all opportunities that Chase eagerly seized to further his goal of creating a new Democratic party based on the exclusion of slavery from the territories. The major role he played at the Free Soil convention in Rochester, which nominated Van Buren for president, testified not only to his perception of a new public issue in the making that was bound to be popular in the North but to his own ambitions for political preferment.

The Whig party in Ohio had been losing ground for several years before the election of 1848. The persistence of hard times during the early 1840s, the seizure by the radical northern Democrats of the free-soil issue in 1846, and then the nomination of Taylor, a southerner and a slaveholder, had injured the party, especially in its former stronghold of transplanted New Englanders in the Western Reserve. Joshua Giddings, the Reserve's most vocal representative, though every bit as opposed to the extension of slavery as Chase, had retained his Whig identity. When Whig unity began to crumble after the presidential election, Giddings found himself unable either to swing his party behind the free-soil movement or to replace Chase as the movement's leader in Ohio.[12]

In a desperate attempt to reclaim its faltering fortunes, the Whig party used its slight majority in the Ohio legislature to gerrymander Hamilton County so that the Whig majority in the countryside surrounding Cincinnati would be represented and not be overwhelmed by the city's Democratic strength. Since the Whigs in the legislature had acted without a quorum, the outraged Democrats throughout the state charged that the law was unconstitutional. The state election of 1848 produced a very nearly equal division between the Democrats and the Whigs, with eleven Free Soilers holding the balance of power in the two houses of the Ohio legislature.[13]

At this point, Chase saw the possibility of his own election to the Senate if he could secure the support of the regular Democrats. Two close associates, Norton S. Townshend, the English-born and largely self-taught physician, and John F. Morse, both Free Soilers and newly elected members of the legislature who were inclined toward the Democratic position on economic questions, worked with Chase to influence their antiextension colleagues. Chase moved in other areas too. He mentioned his availability in veiled but positive terms to Democratic lawyers who, he knew, were leaning toward Free Soil. And he was particularly active in mounting a press campaign that would keep his possible candidacy in the forefront. To that end he used Donn Piatt, a Cincinnati journalist, as a go-between with the Democratic regulars and to author public letters that reviewed Chase's support for Democratic party principles. At the Free Soil convention in Columbus in early December 1848, Chase managed to have the party committed to a program that paralleled the Democratic state platform—a ten-hour law for workers, a thorough revision of the state constitution, condemnation of the Hamilton County apportionment, and currency and banking reform that struck a workable compromise between the hard-money and soft-money factions in the Democratic party.[14]

These propositions, together with secret discussions Chase held with Samuel Medary, former editor of the *Ohio Statesman*, former supporter of Lewis Cass, and patronage-hungry leader of the soft-money Democrats, formed the basis for an alliance between the Free Soilers and the Democrats. Chase was anxious to succeed William Allen, a Van Buren Democrat, whose term in the United States Senate was about to expire. Allen was a candidate for reelection but was unacceptable to the majority Medary group for several reasons, but principally because of his hard-money views. And free-soil-inclined Democrats found him untrustworthy on the slavery issue. Over a period of several weeks Chase and his lieutenants, Morse and Townshend, worked out a complicated deal with Medary in which the Democrats would vote with the Free Soilers for abolition of Ohio's racial discrimination laws, known as the black laws; rescinding the Whig apportionment law for Hamilton County; awarding to Democrats all state partronage, including the printing, judicial appointments, and legislative offices; election of one of Medary's political henchmen, John Breslin, as Speaker of the House; and election of Chase to the United States Senate to replace Allen. With Chase in the background, coaching his Free Soilers, at the American Hotel on High Street opposite the State House, the plan went into effect. But he did not remain for the denouement. By then, Chase had left for home. Potential critics could not say that he was on the scene when he was elected to the United States Senate over Thomas Ewing, the Whig candidate, on February 22, 1849. He had in effect sold the Free Soil party to the Democracy for his own election to the Senate.[15]

At least, this was how Giddings and the Whig free-soilers saw it. John McLean, whose niece was Chase's third wife, regarded Chase's act as not only unconscionable but immoral political treachery. Their personal relations, which had been close for years, were broken at McLean's behest. Though McLean himself was not lacking in political ambition, what he said about Chase was felt by many of Chase's contemporaries. McLean wrote that Chase "is the most unprincipled man politically that I have ever known. He is selfish beyond any other man. And I know from the bargain he has made in being elected to the senate, he is ready to make any bargain to promote his own interest."[16]

This indictment may seem too severe for a political deal that benefited both parties to the agreement. But considering Chase's pretensions to lofty aims and his alliance with such suspect patronage-hungry politicians as Medary, his actions seemed outrageous to most outspoken antislavery men whether of Democratic or Whig antecedents. The free-soil-leaning Democrat Judge Nathaniel Read, a fellow member of the Cincinnati bar, saw the future Chase biographer Robert B. Warden and another young lawyer talking with Chase at the corner of Fifth and Walnut streets in Cincinnati at about this time. After Chase left, Read said to them, "Boys! I see you have been talking with Chase. He is courting you young men. Avoid him. He is a political vampire. No! He's a sort of moral bull-bitch." Among those who remained within the

Whig organization, including the popular young lawyers Rutherford B. Hayes and John Sherman, Chase was regarded as a political pariah. As late as 1852, Horace Greeley was unusually candid in his criticism of Chase's election to the Senate. "It seemed to me," wrote Greeley, "the consummation of the most flagrant conspiracy against law and right."[17] Nor was the regular Democratic organization enthusiastic about Chase for the long run.

Chase's career in the Senate followed a similar antiparty line which he sought to cloak with a pretense of party regularity. When Stephen A. Douglas was about to present the Kansas-Nebraska bill, Chase asked him as an act of courtesy to postpone action for a few days so that he could study the proposal. Douglas agreed. Chase used this time to edit a fierce indictment of the bill that Giddings had written. Other free-soilers, Charles Sumner, Gerrit Smith, and Edward Wade of Ohio, also worked over the draft, but Chase did most of the rewriting. The document, entitled "Appeal to the Independent Democrats," bitterly arraigned Douglas, his position on popular sovereignty, and his explicit repeal of the Missouri Compromise in the bill. The "Appeal" instantly became a public sensation. The high moral ground it took, the reforming zeal that suffused its pages, the position it staked out on the extension of slavery, the mockery it made of popular sovereignty, all contributed to provide a rallying point for both Democrats and Whigs who sought to draw a line against what they perceived as further encroachments of the Slave Power. There was no doubt, however, that Chase double-crossed Douglas. His ends were lofty and consistent, but the timing of the "Appeal" was meant to undercut Douglas and enhance Chase as much as it was to advance the antislavery cause. It has been called, and rightly so, a brilliant piece of propaganda and an effort to exploit a powerful antislavery theme for personal political gain.[18]

This move, and indeed all of Chase's actions while a senator, showed a keen sense of public relations. He was able to justify it in his own mind as furthering the policy program he favored. That it incidentally promoted his own career and his public image as a fearless defender of freedom was simply a means to a worthy end, as he saw it. But his treatment of Douglas added yet another group of important politicians to the growing list of those who did not trust him.

Yet if Chase's sense of timing in the "Appeal" was unfortunate for

Douglas, it crystallized northern public opinion behind Chase. He would be replaced as a senator from Ohio after one term, but the Kansas-Nebraska Act and the beginnings of a civil war in Kansas had finally led to the formation of a new political coalition, the Republican party, based on free soil. Chase's plan to purify the Democratic party had failed, but this new party offered an even better arrangement for his political program in Ohio and throughout the North. Its frankly sectional basis repelled those in the free states who would appease the South on the issue of slavery in the territories.

In 1855, Chase eagerly accepted the Republican nomination for governor of Ohio. In so doing, however, he again added to his list of political enemies. He made a deal with leaders of a new movement, the nativist American or Know-Nothing party, which had suddenly come into prominence partly as a way station for former Whig politicians who had left their own wrecked organization, and partly as a reaction to the influx of immigration following famine and political disturbances in Europe during the late 1840s and early 1850s. Chase had weighed the surging strength of the antislavery movement in Ohio against the reaction of foreign-born voters in Cincinnati and elsewhere. His perception that the one overbalanced the other, especially with no organized Whig party, was accurate. The antislavery and nativist movements were stronger. Many German Protestants and Catholics never forgave Chase for his flirtation with the Know-Nothings. Chase won the election with a fifteen-thousand-vote margin, but he acquired more political enemies.

Although Chase was the only Republican on a ticket of Know-Nothings, their organization did not wholly trust his muted professions of solicitude for their movement, and with good reason. The Know-Nothings made their own nominations; their slate took 8 percent of the vote in the state. In his negotiations with Know-Nothing leaders, Chase had made a deal to back Lewis D. Campbell, a Know-Nothing congressman and a candidate for the speakership, in exchange for his support in the Ohio gubernatorial race. But when Campbell sought Chase's aid in his quest for the speakership, Chase reneged on the deal. Campbell was a contentious person who nevertheless had a strong following among Whig/Republicans and Know-Nothings in Ohio and elsewhere. Chase's failure to honor a commitment added yet another man to the list of those who considered him untrustworthy.[19]

At the time of his greatest triumph as the first Republican governor of the most important and populous western state, a national figure of seemingly transcendent importance, Chase had in effect lost his constituency at home even within his own party. Of course, any politician who aspired to national leadership at this time would experience extreme difficulty in holding together a coalition of the diverse interests, emotional ties and feelings, and personal antagonisms that were bound to arise when new issues and new party organizations were coming into being. But Chase, whose political moves lacked the finesse of a Seward or a Weed, whose personality was stiff, whose ambition was transparent, had sacrificed long-term benefits for immediate goals.

These failings became almost immediately evident when he sought the Republican presidential nomination in Philadelphia in 1856. Although Chase had recognized before any of his rivals that antiforeign sentiment and antislavery were potent if not indispensable issues for success in the North, he was slow to distinguish between the anti-Catholic and antiforeign elements among the nativists. It was difficult to walk the fine line with so many contrary interests involved, but he should have been aware of the surge of anti-Catholicism in his own county. Hayes gave a graphic picture of the situation in the fall of 1854. "Anti-Nebraska, Know-Nothings and general disgust with the powers that be, have carried this county [Hamilton] by between seven and eight thousand majority," he wrote his uncle Sardis Birchard. "How people do hate Catholics and what happiness it was to thousands to have a chance to show it in what seemed a lawful and patriotic manner."[20]

Yet in seeking to capitalize on his thin victory in Ohio, Chase attempted to coordinate antislavery and antiforeign aspects of the new Republican party. This strategy seemed appropriate when the Republicans met at a prenomination convention in Pittsburgh. But Chase's Ohio coalition did not stand up at the first regular Republican convention in Philadelphia. Donn Piatt, the political journalist who helped with Chase's first election to the United States Senate, was on hand to promote Chase with free-soil Democrats. But he and other journalists, with Cincinnati connections, were of little assistance. Former Whig stalwarts and hard-line nativists lined up behind the perpetual presidential candidacy of Supreme Court Justice John McLean to divide the Ohio delegation. For this reason, and because of Chase's blemished record of opportunism, his presumed radicalism on slavery, and particularly his seemingly equivocal record on prohibition and nativism, Chase was passed over for the Republican presidential nomination.[21]

In 1858, Chase was renominated for governor and accepted against his better judgment. Local issues, including the default of more than half a million dollars by the state treasurer, dominated the campaign. The nativists again ran a candidate, indicating a continued distrust of Chase by many of the hard-line antiforeign elements in Ohio. A revitalized Democratic party, aided by substantial federal patronage from the James Buchanan administration and a strong gubernatorial candidate, made the three-cornered race a close one for Chase. His plurality was so thin, some fifteen hundred votes, that his reputation suffered both in the state and among national party leaders. Carl Schurz, the German Protestant leader in the West, for example, though courted by Chase when he visited Columbus in March 1860, would not support him. Seward's strong and consistent antinativist stand made him much more popular than Chase among both German Protestants and Catholics in the West.

But again, in the Chicago convention of 1860, it was the failure of the Ohio delegation to give Chase unanimous support that dealt his candidacy a mortal blow at the outset. This time, Benjamin Wade and the former Whigs in the Ohio delegation split the vote. As Chase complained to his close friend Robert Hosea after the convention, "I do feel the ungenerous conduct of the Ohio delegation and the hardly less ungenerous conduct of those men outside of Ohio, who brought forward the name of Mr. Wade, to divide at home and abroad those who would have supported me, but for this division."[22]

Chase's course up to this point of his career resembled in some respects the picture Shakespeare drew of Bolingbroke in *King Richard II* and in *King Henry IV,* Part One. In Hotspur's words, he was "too indirect for long continuance." Bolingbroke, of course, was successful in securing the crown, but the prize eluded Chase. His career more nearly resembled that of Henry St. John, the early eighteenth-century English politician whom Queen Anne enobled as Viscount Bolingbroke.

Though such analogies are invariably dangerous for speculation, Chase's background and political deviousness do recall this later Bolingbroke's tortuous course. Both men came from aristocratic backgrounds,

Chase from what passed for aristocracy on the New England and western frontier, Bolingbroke from the upper nobility as distinguished from the landed gentry that characterized the class of his great opponent Sir Robert Walpole. Both men were francophiles and fluent in the French language, and both were instinctive critics of a society they regarded as corrupt. Chase was not, like Bolingbroke, seeking to break the power of the gentry and their allies among the city merchants. Quite the reverse; he sought to destroy the great landowners of the South and their system of chattel slavery. There was more of moral uplift to Chase's goals than there ever was to Bolingbroke's. Yet an intrinsic conservatism characterized the thinking of both men, separated as they were by over a century of dramatic change in Western society and by a world of difference in their cultures. There was no patriot king in Chase's worldview, but there was a similar disdain for the easy nostrums of the American Whig party and the dedication of both major parties in the late 1840s and early 1850s to interests rather than to forthright principles of human behavior, as expressed in what they both believed to be enlightened public policy. Whatever their motives, neither man could resist manipulating social institutions like the press to achieve his ends. And their incessant quests for office and for power were perceived, even by their close associates, as character flaws that would not stand close scrutiny.[23]

These political liabilities, arising from his flawed character, prevented Chase from winning the Republican nomination for president either in 1856 or 1860. Despite his sincere commitment to free-soil principles and to the Constitution, Chase's personality and background cost him the trust of his political associates and, as a consequence, the opportunity to become the first Republican president.

NOTES

1. J. W. Schuckers, *Life and Public Services of Salmon Portland Chase* (New York: D. Appleton, 1874), p. 27.

2. S. P. Chase, Diary, July 4, 1830, Salmon P. Chase Papers, Library of Congress (LC).

3. Chase to Charles D. Cleveland, August 13, 1832, Salmon P. Chase Papers, Historical Society of Pennsylvania (HSP); Printed circular, Chase Papers, LC;

Robert Warden, *An Account of the Private Life and Public Services of Salmon Portland Chase* (Cincinnati: Wilstach, Baldwin & Co., 1874), pp. 250–51.

4. Chase, Diary, March 13, 1841, LC; *Cincinnati Daily Gazette,* April 7, 13, 1841.

5. Schuckers, *Life of Chase,* pp. 35–36; Charles Richard Williams, ed., *Diary and Letters of Rutherford Birchard Hayes,* 5 vols. (Columbus: Ohio State Archeological and Historical Society, 1922), 1: 384.

6. Frederick J. Blue, *Salmon P. Chase: A Life in Politics* (Kent, Ohio: Kent State University Press, 1987), p. 42; Chase to John T. Trowbridge, January 25, 1864, Salmon P. Chase Papers, Cincinnati Historical Society; Philander Chase to Baruch Chase, July 31, 1823, Salmon P. Chase Papers, New Hampshire Antiquarian Society.

7. Francis P. Weisberger, *The Passing of the Frontier, 1825–1850* (Columbus: Ohio State Archaeological and Historical Society, 1941), pp. 376–79.

8. Chase addressed the convention and declared that he was for free trade. See Warden, *Chase,* p. 299; *Philanthropist,* January 12, 1842.

9. Chase to Smith, May 14, 1842, Gerrit Smith Papers, Syracuse University; Henry B. Stanton to Chase, February 6, 1844, Chase Papers, LC.

10. Dwight L. Dumond, ed., *Letters of James Gillespie Birney, 1831–1857,* 2 vols. (1938; rpt. Gloucester, Mass.: Peter Smith, 1966), 2: 887; Chase to John P. Hale, May 12, 1847, John P. Hale Papers, New Hampshire Historical Society.

11. Gerrit Smith, "To the Liberty Party," May 7, 1846, printed circular, Chase Papers, HSP.

12. Stephen Maizlish, *The Triumph of Sectionalism: The Transformation of Ohio Politics* (Kent, Ohio: Kent State University Press, 1983), pp. 63–64.

13. Ibid., pp. 117–20.

14. Weisberger, *Passing of the Frontier,* pp. 471–72; Warden, *Chase,* pp. 328–29.

15. Maizlish, *Triumph of Sectionalism,* chap. 6; Richard H. Sewell, *Ballots for Freedom: Antislavery Politics in the United States, 1837–1860* (New York: Oxford University Press, 1976), pp. 206–7.

16. Quoted in Francis P. Weisberger, *The Life of John McLean* (Columbus: Da Capo, 1937), p. 214.

17. Warden, *Chase,* p. 329; Williams, ed., *Diary and Letters of Hayes,* 1: 489; John Sherman, *Recollections of Forty Years in the House, Senate and Cabinet,* 2 vols. (Chicago: Werner Company, 1895), 1: 106–7; Greeley to Chase, April 16, 1852, Chase Papers, HSP.

18. Michael F. Holt, *The Political Crisis of the 1850s* (New York: Wiley, 1978), pp. 152–53; William E. Gienapp, *The Origins of the Republican Party, 1852–1856* (New York: Oxford University Press, 1987), pp. 71–75.

19. Maizlish, *Triumph of Sectionalism,* p. 233; William E. Gienapp, "Nativism

and the Creation of a Republican Majority in the North before the Civil War," *Journal of American History* 72 (1985): 540–43; Gienapp, *Origins of the Republican Party*, pp. 241–42.

20. Williams, ed., *Diary and Letters of Hayes*, 1: 471.

21. Warden, *Chase*, pp. 328–29.

22. Chase to Robert Hosea, June 5, 1860, Chase Papers, LC.

23. See revisionist views of Bolingbroke in Isaac Kramnick, *Bolingbroke and His Circle: The Politics of Nostalgia in the Age of Walpole* (Cambridge, Mass.: Harvard University Press, 1968), and Jeffrey Hart, *Viscount Bolingbroke: Tory Humanist* (London: Routledge & Kegan Paul, 1965). The traditional Whig view of Bolingbroke is best expressed in Walter Bagehot's essay, "Bolingbroke as a Statesman," in Norman St. John-Stevas, ed., *Bagehot's Historical Essays* (Garden City, N.Y.: Anchor Books, 1965), pp. 1–42.

★

CHAPTER THREE

LINCOLN AND THE RHETORIC

OF POLITICS

★

PHILLIP S. PALUDAN

In the introduction to *The Politics of Union,* James A. Rawley notes, "Diversity of outlook offered energy and vitality to Northern politics. Civil War politics accommodated and even exploited with great success the natural tensions of the hour, invigorating the war effort instead of debilitating it."[1] This insight offered in his usual lean and careful prose provides a text that I want to explicate. I do not fully agree with it, but as is usual in Rawley's work, he sets the idea forward in a way that encourages thought and discussion. We are grateful to him not only for the substantial contributions he has made to our understanding of the Civil War era but also for a manner of discourse which promotes an ongoing conversation about it.

Rawley's style as well as the substance of his work help us to keep in mind a crucial fact about the writing of history. The past is always too large and too complex for final conclusions by historians. The history that humankind has lived is a complex narrative. Our analyses must always be provisional. The past we study is larger and better than the analyses we provide of it. The story of that past lives on, provoking future analyses and assessments but transcending them all, and hence keeps the debate and argument, or maybe even the conversation, going over the meaning and the nature of the nation's past and thus its present and future.[2]

This chapter is an effort to keep that conversation going. The subject is interdisciplinary in nature. In talking about Abraham Lincoln and the rhetoric of politics I want to stress that constitutional issues gave politics its structure. In so doing I will examine the substance of constitutional discussion, but, more important, I will focus on its style. The question is, How did people talk about the Constitution and how did the way they talked, especially the way Lincoln talked, help or hinder the successful working of the political and constitutional system?

Rawley has hit upon a crucial point in emphasizing the value of diversity. My objection is really a gloss on that fact, for I think that if we look at the style in which that diversity was expressed we will discover costs as well as benefits. Proving that assertion requires a voyage beyond the usual borders of historiography. I am aware that ancient mapmakers used to write in areas not yet explored, "Here there be tigers."

I am at best a journeyman in the fields of hermeneutics and political philosophy. But the benefits for historical study that can come from these fields may compensate for my limitations. I offer these ideas in a spirit that echoes James Boyd White's urging that law be seen not as the authoritative and final declaration of the sovereign but as an offer to converse and learn by presenting an agenda for discussion.[3]

One of the problems is that the dominant style of scholarship, the very way we present what we do, at times obstructs conversation. We describe what we do as "scholarly argument" or "scholarly debate." We write our books and articles as revisions, and the mode is of truth replacing error. I am reminded of the biblical phraseology, "You have heard it said in days of old . . . but verily I say unto you. . . ." Whatever may be said for this mode in professional terms, in stimulating historiography and conferences, for example, it does not look much like a conversation. It lacks the tone of a discussion in which all parties wish the process to go on and on with increased and integrated understanding emerging. I sometimes think that the scholar defines a discussion as having two parts: part 1, talking; part 2, waiting to talk.

Existing scholarship has provided intriguing insights on Lincoln and the Constitution. From careful studies of particular constitutional provisions to more general pictures of the constitutional system as a whole, scholars have contributed to the debate about Lincoln. These works reflect the broad argument over whether Lincoln supported or assailed the Constitution, whether it is narrowly or broadly understood. The verdict is that Lincoln was right, his opponents wrong.

On balance, I agree with the prevailing view. I believe that if we need verdicts, the current one is correct. But I want to step outside that debate and move toward conversation. In doing so, I want to contribute to the work of other scholars but also to do something which I think might open up new questions about Lincoln. Opening new questions is what the best conversation is all about. As Hans George Gadamer says, "The art of questioning is the art of being able to ask further questions, that is, it is also the art of thought. It is called dialectic because it is the art of carrying on a real conversation."[4]

I want to open the conversation in four parts. The first is to argue for the value of seeing the constitutional system as a conversation. Here I will appeal to the authority of recent thinking on that system. Then I want to show how Lincoln understood the system as requiring a conversation between two fundamental documents, the Constitution and the Declaration of Independence. Here the form will be to provide a story and an argument. Then I will work from the premise that conversation as an idea allows us to look at style as well as substance, the way something is said as well as what is said. Here I will argue that Lincoln at first subordinated the traditional southern style of describing the world, one characterized by the story. As he sought to rise from his southern roots, he adopted a style more in conformity with the modernizing North, the style of analysis and argument, which emphasized mind, reason, and control. His use of this style, in the context of a culture already polarized in religion and politics, both advanced and retarded the constitutional conversation. In the last section of this all-too-simple overview I will assert that Lincoln rediscovered story as a way of comprehending the world and put story into conversation with argument. As he did this, he reclaimed a southern heritage, developed a subtle and complex religious perspective, and reconstituted the republic.

The definition of conversation suggests the power of the term as a metaphor. Although we now think of conversation as describing the act of exchanging ideas and opinions, the term originally referred to the context in which this talking took place. The word comes from the Latin *conversatio,* meaning a frequent abode, intercourse, a manner of life, a social circle. Thomas Shelton says, "You may know the man by the conversation he keeps."[5] In the eighteenth century a portrait of a group of notables was called a conversation piece. That did not mean something for the viewer to talk about. It meant that in the picture men were together among those with whom they had their social being.

Some authors have enlarged the importance of the idea by declaring that human beings are defined by their encounters with others and with the world. The German poet Friedrich Hölderlin speaks of "the conversation that we are"—a position Martin Heidegger adopts in arguing that human beings are nothing more than a conversation.[6] This suggests to me that the idea of conversation speaks to profound issues having to do with a person's relations with the world and with other human beings, hence with the issue of law, and hence with Lincoln and the Constitution.

This idea is not, I regret to say, wholly original. James Boyd White says that the structure of the Constitution can best be understood as "a rhetorical text: as establishing a set of roles, speakers, topics and occasions for speech. So understood many of its ambiguities and uncertainties become more comprehensible; we can see it as attempting to establish a conversation of a certain kind, and its ambiguities as ways of at once defining and leaving open the topics of the conversation." Sotirios Barber argues that the basic vision of the Constitution is of an ongoing conversation: "At the center of what the Constitution envisions are men and women whose desire for the best conceptions of the Constitution and the good society moves them to self-criticism and an antipathy to everything that stands in the way of giving and exchanging reasons with each other about how to live and what to believe." What is most important here, I think, is that a constitution, to remain vital in the face of change, must keep its conversation going; it must redefine the meaning of words like liberty, equality, and due process; it must balance the voices and claims of states and nation, maintaining the dialogue between branches of government. It must, in Justice Oliver Wendell Holmes's words, describe "things" and not unchangeable "words." Words have to lose their meaning and be redefined as the law of the Constitution is applied to changing needs. And keeping debate and discussion going on is crucial to keeping the Constitution alive.[7]

Lincoln usually worked the constitutional system with a fine sensitivity to the importance of such conversations. His working with Congress to resolve vital wartime issues usually revealed the mutual respect of a partnership in handling affairs of state. The proper picture of that story is not of Lincoln *or* Congress prevailing but of the maintenance of the dialogue between them. He also was a master of balancing Republican factions. These topics deserve more extensive discussion than can be provided here. My focus is Lincoln's constitutional thought, on the ideas that inspired and shaped his behavior.

Fundamental to his thought, I believe, was his understanding of the conversation between the Declaration and the Constitution. I emphasize that the heart was the conversation between the two. If we recognize that, we can escape another argument among historians.

In recent years we have argued over whether Lincoln was a conservative or a revolutionary. Much of that argument has hinged on whether we emphasize the Declaration or the Constitution, Lincoln's devotion to the equality of men or his commitment to saving the Constitution and the Union. The authoritative *Abraham Lincoln Encyclopedia* illustrates the dichotomy: "As an antislavery man, Lincoln had a natural affinity not for the Constitution (with its compromising protections of the slave interest) but for the Declaration of Independence."[8]

A key document in this discussion has been Lincoln's fragment on the Constitution in which he said that the Declaration was the "apple of gold" and the Constitution and Union the "*picture* of *silver*." The frame existed for the apple, not the other way around. If we stop there, as many scholars do, we choose the Declaration. But Lincoln did not stop there. He went on to say, "So let us act that neither *picture*, [n]or *apple* shall ever be blurred, or bruised or broken." It seems that Lincoln thought the two were interrelated, one necessary to the other.[9]

Lincoln's view of the Declaration and the Constitution envisioned an unfolding conversation between the two which would ultimately bring about a more perfect Union. As a young man, Lincoln did not understand this very well, but in the environment produced by the Nebraska crisis he figured it out.

The young Lincoln focused on law and order, the constitutional system and the style of thinking that emphasized its legal structure. The address at the Lyceum in January 1838 cataloged attacks on order, warned against mob rule, and urged that citizens make obedience to law "the political religion of the nation." He insisted that this could be done only if "cold, calculating unimpassioned reason . . . furnished all the materials of our future defense and support." Either "all conquering mind," as he would call it in the address to the Temperance Society, had to dominate, or the founder's dream would flee.

We are now looking not only at substance but at style, the style that Lincoln thought was imperative to save the nation. In these early addresses we see the young professional lawyer at work. He had joined the bar less than a year before he spoke at the Lyceum. With the passion of a novitiate, he espoused legal ideals and even emphasized the need for citizens of the republic to think like lawyers: rational, precise, following and respecting system and order. Personal factors seem to have been important here. He had escaped the rude rural southern environment with its interest in nonrational things, its organic interconnections, its storylike environs. He substituted argument and mind for story and sentiment. Men who controlled themselves needed to counter the commonplace passions of much of the backward democracy. He never wanted to slide back into that dirt-farmer world again. Both his style and substance revealed that fear.[10]

As he grew older, Lincoln developed a less rigid, *substantive* perspective on the law. In the midst of the crisis over slavery he began to evolve a picture of a changing constitutional system, which moved beyond mere respect for every law with the passion of a religion. Here I will highlight only the major elements of that evolution.

First, Lincoln became aware that the Constitution harbored elements that undercut the constitutional system. He recognized that originally slavery had been the price of union and of the Constitution. Unless slavery was admitted into the founding document, there would have been nothing to found. But rather than insist on rigid respect for all the laws, as the young lawyer of 1838 had done, he began to protest how much respecting the laws cost the conscience. In his August 1855 letter to his old friend Joshua Speed, for example, he protested: "You ought . . . to appreciate how much the great body of the Northern people do crucify their feelings, in order to maintain their loyalty to the consitution and the Union." And he declared that the Nebraska business was a violation of law, not just in a technical sense but in replacing the legal order with violence. Lincoln felt so passionately about this that he resorted to hyperbole beyond what an "all conquering mind" might have tolerated. He equated the physical violence of Missouri border ruffians with "violent disagreement" between lawmakers and the people. He proclaimed, "The slave-breeders and slave-traders . . . [though] a small odious and detested class . . . in politics dictate the course of all of you, and are as completely your masters, as you are the masters of your own negroes." Clearly, Lincoln was deeply disturbed over the constitutional contradictions and complexities generated by the Nebraska question.[11]

Part of his passion arose from his anger at threats to the legal system. Lincoln shared the feelings of growing numbers of jurists and legal thinkers that the defenders of slavery were stifling constitutional freedoms. He protested to Speed that the proslavery legislature of Kansas provided the death penalty for people who spoke to slaves about their rights. He attacked the *Dred Scott* decision for, among other things, foreclosing debate on the issue of slavery in the territories. And in March 1860 he complained that supporters of slavery did not want their institution discussed in pulpits or in tract societies or in politics, not in the slave states or in the free states. The constitutional protection for slavery eroded civil liberties. One element in the Constitution threatened another. All these questions were in Lincoln's mind at the very time when he was paying increasing attention to the Declaration of Independence. The apple and the picture were both under consideration.[12]

The Declaration got most of the attention in the post-Nebraska days. It provided the fundamental idea of equality on which the entire system rested. But Lincoln insisted that the authors of the Constitution had not repudiated the Declaration. Rather, they had established a way for freedom to move forward. The territorial clause gave Congress the power to vote slavery in or out of the territories. The founders' ideal had been to vote it out as soon as possible. They had "declare[d] the right [of equality] so that *enforcement* of it might follow as fast as circumstances should permit."[13]

Yet the Declaration was not self-executing. Its principle of equality was the apple of gold. But the Union and the Constitution that framed it existed not to conceal or destroy the apple but to "*adorn,* and *preserve* it." The principle required a constitution and union that adorned and preserved the ideal of equality, not a choice between Constitution and Union, on one side, and Declaration on the other.[14]

Lincoln never asked anyone to make such a choice. He seems to have thought of the two documents almost as one. He put them in the same historical moment. The 1776 Philadelphia meeting was not discussed separately from that of 1787. He never seems to have suggested that the Constitution with its eight provisions protecting slavery was a major retreat from the equality of the Declaration. He gave both the same authorship and thereby inferred that the intentions of the framers remained the same in the eleven years from 1776 to 1787. Even when he became more sensitive to the fact that protecting slavery meant threatening other constitutional provisions, Lincoln did not throw out the baby with the bathwater. He did not take the path of William Lloyd Garrison and his associates in calling the entire Constitution an agreement with hell. He did not burn the Constitution; he worked to make the picture adorn and preserve the apple of gold. He wanted to keep the conversation between the fundamental documents alive—to keep the process evolving.

Lincoln's commitment to evolution was clear in his idea of what the Declaration meant. He insisted that the ideal of equality was open-ended. He deplored Stephen A. Douglas's vision of the Declaration as justifying only separation from England. That idea killed the promises of equality and made the document a dead proclamation. But the equality it had promised abided. It was not a dead declaration. It was a living promise, "a standard maxim [to be] . . . constantly looked to, constantly labored for and even though never perfectly attained, constantly approximated, and thereby constantly spreading and deepening its influence, and augmenting the happiness and value of life to all people of all colors everywhere." When at Gettysburg he exhorted the nation to achieve the ideals of four score and seven years before, he also showed his belief in a process. The new nation was dedicated, not to the immutable certainty but to the "*proposition*" that all men were created equal. The main ideal of equality had to be discussed and considered and kept as a question, not a statement, an ideal that was vital enough to sustain, to demand an abiding conversation, a conversation made possible by the Union and the political-constitutional system.[15]

Lincoln's belief in an abiding and evolving Constitution was demonstrated by his self-proclaimed and continued devotion to it, his belief in its adaptability to the demands of war, and his advocacy of an amendment to remove the cold hand of slavery from its body, thus harmonizing the two documents and the order and liberty they represented. No longer would slavery "force . . . so many really good men amongst ourselves into an open war with the very fundamental principles of civil liberty—criticizing the Declaration of Independence." Any government dedicated to the proposition that all men are created equal deserved to abide, deserved increased devotion, and deserved not to perish from the earth.[16]

He believed in an evolving Declaration and an evolving Constitution. He also believed in preserving the environment of the conversation, the electoral process established as the means of changing governments under the Constitution. Lincoln's devotion to the system itself was thunderingly shown in his determination to save the electoral process by fighting four long years in its behalf. This did not necessarily mean that Lincoln had great faith in democracy, but that must be another story.

Lincoln wanted to maintain the apple and the picture, and he saw them as interconnected. That seems to be the most important quality of his constitutional thought. He wanted the two documents, born of the same ideals, men, and times, to maintain the conversation over the relationship between law and liberty in this nation.

Much of the foregoing account is familiar in its parts, perhaps even in its whole. But the metaphor of conversation can perhaps open new territory. For conversation has style as well as substance. Any time we deal with conversation we become alert to language and hence to style of communication as well as, perhaps more than, substance! A way of speaking shapes the experience of listeners; it also shapes that of the speaker. It describes how one sees the world and wishes it to be seen by listeners and readers.[17]

Looking at how Lincoln sustained his positions will help us understand better how he understood the constitutional conversation, and that may help explain why he apparently stopped the conversation during the war. That in turn is wrapped up in another concept arising from viewing Lincoln in relation to his rhetoric—his transition from story to argument and then back to story. This understanding might help reveal the "conversation" that went on within Lincoln, making him the man he was always becoming.

Although Lincoln evolved a vision of law as a system that secured an open discussion and realization of its fundamental ideas, he did not in the prewar years abandon the style he had adopted when he left behind his poor, rural, southern heritage and joined the profession of law. He insisted that the dialogue of the polity had to conform to the ideal of legal thought—mind, "all conquering mind," with its capacity for distinguishing and developing a logically structured understanding or argument, had to prevail or disorder and anarchy would conquer. In short, he clung to argument as a style, a way of understanding and responding to the disunion crisis that undercut many of the ideals he advocated as ends.[18]

The public legal system is adversarial. It rests on the premise that truth will emerge from combat in which two adversaries do their best to sustain their versions of the truth. Perhaps in an ideal forum, where the law is seen as a conversation rather than as the authoritative will of the state, the legal system can operate as a conversation. But that involves a commitment by parties to act in such a way that the meaning of the law is discovered, not that one side or another should win. When what Judge Jerome Frank termed the "fight theory of justice" occurs, winning takes over from truth-finding. And the adversaries behave as though they believe that they understand the truth, that their reasoning and fact-gathering describe the way the world is.[19]

Lincoln was a lawyer and shared this adversarial perspective. He was also a politician at a time when politics was passionate and polar. Voters in the mid-nineteenth century flocked to the polls in spectacular numbers. An 80 percent turnout of eligible voters was not unusual. And voters' loyalty was legendary. Parties lost not when voters crossed party lines to vote for the opposition, but when their own people stayed home. Few people could stomach voting for someone in the enemy party. Lincoln was proudly a party man, first a Whig and then a Republican at a time when the culture of politics demanded polarized rhetoric. His twin professions of lawyer and politician forged in Lincoln an adversarial style.

Religion in antebellum America further encouraged Manichean visions. The Second Great Awakening had revived American Christianity to a militance that would send Christian soldiers with the cross of Jesus to fight for both North and South. It also divided politics along religious lines with Catholics the special targets of angry, self-righteous Protestants. Lincoln abhorred nativism, and his religious persuasion emphasized the doctrine of fate, not self-righteousness. But the audiences he addressed most often perceived right and wrong in either/or terms and hence furthered the adversarial style of political discourse. Lincoln thus was disposed by his twin occupations toward a rhetoric of polarities, of either/or, of argument. The religious perspective of his audience added to this disposition.

This adversarial worldview served a positive purpose as a means to keep the constitutional conversation alive. It was imperative in the debates with Stephen Douglas, who was speaking for powerful forces loose in the land. He spoke for a Jacksonian democracy, which extolled the will of the people and gloried in the expansion of mass democracy across the continent. Yet it was a movement that denied the humanity and the right to equal liberty of Indians and blacks. When Jacksonians took over in the free states, they took away the rights of free blacks as quickly as they justified confiscating Indian land. And they protected slavery with a desperate passion. This tyrannical form of American majoritarian democracy also underlay the burgeoning Know-Nothing movement, despite its Whig-Republican origin. The momentum of Douglas's Jacksonianism and the forum in which he spoke demanded the sense of certainty, the unalloyed assertion of moral superiority of the adversarial style. Lawyer Lincoln marshaled the argument powerfully for the centrality of the Declaration and the ideals of equality in the political and constitutional system. Lincoln here was appealing beyond the mere force of history in the constitutional system to constitutional aspirations that spoke of what the system reached for, not what it grasped.[20]

Both Lincoln's style and substance divided the house. He spoke of understanding the circumstances of slaveowners, claiming that northerners in southern circumstances would probably also defend the evil system of human bondage. But he made the case for equalitarian ideals, against Douglas's Burkean image of a culture whose way of life should not be disrupted by mere abstractions. The style forged images of right versus wrong, and Lincoln asked for faith that right would make might and bring victory. The tug had to come and, he believed, better now than later.

The adversarial style also nourished the constitutional conversation in the secession crisis. A real divided house now put all constitutional questions in adversarial terms. Lincoln's brief for perpetual union, although rather unsophisticated and perhaps erroneous historically, made a persuasive case for why the Union was worth saving and why the southern constitutional argument destroyed, rather than fulfilled, constitutional fate. Lincoln was not recreating a historical reality. He was trying to create a rhetorical reality that would inspire saving the constitutional Union.[21]

Similarly, the adversarial style Lincoln had mastered served the system itself in the early debate with Roger Taney over suspension of the privilege of the writ of habeas corpus in the border areas. He had able cocounsel here. Two professors of constitutional law at Harvard, the best constitutional lawyer in Congress, the editor of the important *Harper's Weekly,* and others sustained Lincoln's position. Taney's argument, narrowly focused on one question of whether Congress or the president had the power to suspend, had some validity. But Lincoln's answer had similar technical strength, and it was much stronger when looked at from a larger systematic position.[22]

Yet in the interest of the scholarly conversation on Lincoln, we should note also that this style sometimes provided fuel for his enemies past and present. Dialectic demands not only that we show the weakness in the opponent's position, thus balancing inquiry. It demands that we bring out its real strength so that we can determine what more needs to be said.

Surely Lincoln's enthusiasm for victory and his adversarial style led him beyond at least fairness at times in the debates with Douglas. The story that Roger Taney, James Buchanan, Franklin Pierce, and Stephen Douglas were conspiring to introduce slavery not only to the territories but into free states is the triumph of debate tactics over complex reality. Yes, he said, getting a little adversarial himself, a legal argument could be made which traveled via dicta in *Strader* through dicta and opinion in *Dred Scott* to some future case. But for that hypothetical prospect to become reality, would not *Taney's* Supreme Court have to have overturned *Barron* v. *Baltimore* and thus *nationalized* the Bill of Rights?[23]

Lincoln the advocate also went beyond necessity and hence at least clouded honest dialogue in his treatments of civil liberty issues in the nonborder North. Although Lincoln may have had suspicions about the so-called Northwest conspiracy, he and his administration did little to inhibit prosecution of the comic opera conspirators in the Midwest. Two days after issuing the controversial preliminary Emancipation Proclamation, he suspended the privilege of the writ of habeas corpus throughout the North. Decisions concerning who could say what about the administration's policy were thus in the hands of military officers, the Ambrose Burnsides of the North.[24]

Furthermore, Lincoln did nothing to limit public anxiety about the extent of suppression by his administration. Montgomery Blair in the Post Office Department had almost carte blanche to control the mails, and William Seward, then Edwin Stanton, followed a policy of arresting some individuals to intimidate others. Lincoln did not explain, as Mark Neely has done, that many of the arrests had nothing to do with antigovernment protest. He encouraged people to believe that Seward's and then Stanton's "little bell" rang a great deal to silence large numbers of critics. Did he intend to have a "chilling effect" on debate during the war? He could not have been ignorant of that possibility. His definitions of what behavior might be dangerous were sweeping and conceded nothing material. His letters to Erastus Corning and then to the Ohio Democrats marshaled a legal argument about which, it seems, even he had some doubts, though he never openly confessed them.

Lincoln's defense suggests that he knew he endangered parts for the whole. He spoke of amputating a limb to save the body, strong medicines for the sick which are unsuitable for the healthy, one law sacrificed so that "all the laws but one" might be saved. Yet he denied breaking even one law. He betrayed an extreme view of who was dangerous. He said that insurgents had been planning rebellion for thirty years and had relied on aiders and abettors to raise constitutional issues to advance the rebellion. Not only were vocal protests potentially helpful to the enemy; even silence was suspect, for "the man who stands by and says nothing, when the peril of his government is discussed cannot be misunderstood. If not hindered he is sure to help the enemy."[25]

When those who raised legitimate constitutional concerns were accused of abetting rebellion for decades, and silence implied sedition, it became understandable that even his own supporters protested the administration's stance. Horace Greeley declared that "freedom of speech and of the press are rights which like everything else have their limitations. The license of speech and of the press which men like Vallandigham engage in calls for abridgment of neither." The editor of *Harper's Weekly* wrote, "The mistake of the government [was in] not trusting the people sufficiently." They had "quite enough courage to bear any amount of misfortune and quite sense enough to understand any amount of seditious nonsense be it uttered ever so glibly." Many of the jurists who supported Lincoln in 1861 had abandoned him by late 1862. Harvard's Joel Parker began to call the Lincoln government (with similar adversarial passion) "a perfect military despotism."[26]

Lincoln's justification, that he was protecting the entire system, provides a beginning point for discussion, not the end as some scholars have made it. Some speech does endanger conversation. Charges that those with different ideas are parts of a conspiracy or are dictators are two prime examples. But these facts do not answer the question of whether the overall system was endangered by the activities he suppressed or allowed to be suppressed. We need to provide questions for Lincoln, not merely justifying statements.[27]

One of the more promising starting points for asking those questions regards Lincoln's experience with and devotion to legal advocacy as a way of describing reality. It was a perspective that had formed a vital part of his escape from childhood ignorance and deprivation to the competence and influence of adulthood. The disunion crisis certainly called for advocacy, but in addition, Lincoln's personal history meant that man and moment had met and that there were costs as well as benefits in the meeting.

But Lincoln had another voice, another way of viewing the world, a form often in conversation with advocacy, but a more integrating and authentic way of viewing the world. This was story, the form he had absorbed in his early southern culture, the style that fit his own religious perspective, provided him relaxation, and ultimately the instrument he used to reconstitute the constitutional system.[28] "I have Boston cousins," the southern writer Flannery O'Connor said once, "and when they come South they discuss problems, they don't tell stories. We tell sto-ries."[29]

The difference between discussing problems and telling stories is complex. A story can describe someone discussing a problem, analyzing an issue, or advocating a viewpoint. The discussion of a problem can involve telling a story. But the key distinction is the overall purpose for choosing the approach to understanding. In solving problems one tells a story to prove a point, to make a case. Problems elicit analysis, distinc-tions, categorization. But telling a story evokes wholes, contexts, con-tingencies, interconnections. Discussing problems may be distinguished from storytelling by the amount of metaphor that is expected, the numbers of meanings that one includes. Storytelling at its best seeks many shadings, many meanings, many textures. Problem discussion requires distinguishing meanings and eliminating textures and nuance. Making these distinctions puts the analyst in control of the topic, the problem. The analyst shapes what we understand and what is relevant. But in storytelling the use of metaphors brings into being a range of possible understanding that may be much more than the teller of the tale imagines.[30]

Lincoln had confronted the problem of the place of equality in the constitutional Union with keen analysis and powerful logic. He pro-vided persuasive briefs for his position. But as the war moved inexora-bly, uncontrollably on, he seems to have become aware of the inade-quacy of that form. He confessed that events had controlled him and thereby undercut the advocate's assumption that her or his logical pre-sentation of and argument for a particular picture of experience was right. "What I deal in is too vast for malicious dealing," he said, and thus undercut the sense of righteousness that pervaded the fight theory of justice.[31]

Toward the end he was describing the war in a transcendent story, which he had not created, but which shaped and molded him and the nation he wanted to save. The Second Inaugural Address perhaps best revealed the new direction. It diminished advocacy in tone, in sub-stance, and in style. It expanded the storylike understanding that had remained part of him as well. In the opening paragraphs Lincoln sug-gested that argument was less appropriate than in 1861. He would not provide an extended address or a detailed statement. The people knew these arguments as well as they knew the course of the war. It was time to move beyond argument.

Still, the adversarial mode remained. Insurgents, Lincoln said, plotted destruction of the Union even as he sought to save it in 1861, and they were the ones who would make war. The insurgents wanted to expand slavery, the government only to restrict its expansion. Yet as Lincoln proceeded, argument became the minor key, and Lincoln here presented a story of the conflict that made debate almost irrelevant. For the conflict between the sections had been motivated not by human adversaries but by some higher plan. Human understandings had to be mitigated with the recognition that God's judgment was on both sides and "the Almighty has His own purposes" and those purposes made the arguments of the adversaries minor factors. God was punishing both sides with a "fundamental and astounding" bloody war. Human judgments of right and wrong were to be replaced with charity, with such firmness in the right as could be commensurate with what God allowed humans to see and understand.

The Second Inaugural Address did not mark the replacement in Lincoln's thought of argument by story. Both voices were there. Lincoln was in process himself, now finding story more appropriate than argument, subordinating the righteous advocate to the humble participant within the larger story. An "all conquering mind" proved too one-sided; now the story of mind's limitations reemerged. But the dialogue between the two was now alive. The divided house had justified advocacy and appealed to the public Lincoln's professional disposition for it. But the war had become too complex, too astounding, for him to believe that mere argument made complete sense. The dialogue of story with argument now made its appearance. The conversation not just between liberty and order, the Declaration and the Constitution, but between ways of understanding the nation and the meaning of its history began to be rediscovered.

Lincoln was moving beyond "pernicious abstraction" to the humility that came after "all conquering mind" had shown its limitations. He now aspired perhaps to having men recognize that they did not know enough to close the conversation. The arrogance of reason which thinks it has the answers was to be informed by an understanding that the story of the nation was still unfolding and was being written in ways that only

God could understand. Lincoln seems to have been suggesting that doing justice and loving mercy might very well depend, in a constitutional sense, on walking humbly before God, on not knowing answers, but wondering about the questions. That, in my judgment, is something worth having a conversation about.

NOTES

1. James A. Rawley, *The Politics of Union* (Lincoln: University of Nebraska Press, 1974), p. 3.

2. James Wiggins notes that "stories that matter are greater than and outlive their interpretations" ("Within and without Stories," in Wiggins, ed., *Religion as Story* [New York: Harper & Row, 1974], p. 19).

3. James Boyd White, *When Words Lose Their Meaning: Constitutions and Reconstitutions of Language, Character and Community* (Chicago: University of Chicago Press, 1984); White, *Heracles' Bow: Essays on the Rhetoric and Poetics of the Law* (Madison: University of Wisconsin Press, 1985); Sotirios Barber, *On What the Constitution Means* (Baltimore: Johns Hopkins University Press, 1984); Allan C. Hutchinson, "From Cultural Construction to Historical Deconstruction," *Yale Law Journal* 94 (1984), 209–37; Ronald Dworkin, *Law's Empire* (Cambridge, Mass.: Harvard University Press, 1986).

4. Hans George Gadamer, *Truth and Method,* ed. Garrett Barden and John Cumming (New York: Seabury Press, 1975), p. 331, as quoted in Joel C. Weinsheimer, *Gadamer's Hermeneutics: A Reading of Truth and Method* (New Haven: Yale University Press, 1985), pp. 206–12.

5. *Oxford English Dictionary* (New York: Oxford University Press, 1978), 2:941.

6. Lon L. Fuller, *The Morality of Law* (New Haven: Yale University Press, 1969), pp. 184–86; Weinsheimer, *Gadamer's Hermeneutics,* p. 213.

7. White, *When Words Lose Their Meaning;* Barber, *On What the Constitution Means.*

8. Mark E. Neely, *The Abraham Lincoln Encyclopedia* (New York: McGraw-Hill, 1982), p. 70. Harry Jaffa, *Crisis of the House Divided: An Interpretation of the Issues in the Lincoln-Douglas Debates* (Chicago: University of Chicago Press, 1982), chap. 15, is the most extensive argument dividing Lincoln the supporter of the Declaration from Douglas the proponent of the Constitution. See also Gary J. Jacobsohn, "Abraham Lincoln 'On This Question of Judicial Authority': The Theory of Constitutional Aspiration," *Western Political Quarterly* 36 (1984): 52–70, for the most recent example of side choosing. The clash over conservative or revolu-

tionary Lincoln can be seen in Phillip S. Paludan, "Lincoln, the Rule of Law and the American Revolution," *Journal of the Illinois State Historical Society* 70 (1977): 10–17, for the conservative Lincoln, and Otto Olsen, "Abraham Lincoln as Revolutionary," *Civil War History* 24 (1978): 213–24. See James McPherson, "Abraham Lincoln and the Second American Revolution," in John Thomas, ed., *Abraham Lincoln and the American Political Tradition* (Amherst: University of Massachusetts Press, 1986), for an overview of the clash and an argument that splits the difference by arguing that Lincoln was conservative but open to the demands of the era for revolutionary change. Note that Lincoln almost always said *Constitution* and *Union* in the same phrase. The two seem intertwined in his mind. It would be interesting to look at the conversation between these two concepts in Lincoln's thought. Herman Belz, "Lincoln and the Constitution: The Dictatorship Question Reconsidered" (Ft. Wayne: Louis Warren Library and Museum, 1984), points to a beginning for that inquiry.

9. Roy P. Basler, ed., *The Collected Works of Abraham Lincoln,* 9 vols. (New Brunswick: Rutgers University Press, 1953–55), 4: 168–69 (ca. January 1861).

10. See Stephan B. Oates, *With Malice toward None: The Life of Abraham Lincoln* (New York: Mentor, 1977), for Lincoln as aspiring professional. George Fredrickson, "The Search for Order and Community," in G. Cullom Davis et al., eds., *The Public and Private Lincoln* (Carbondale: Southern Illinois University Press, 1979), puts Lincoln among the legal profession seeking to restrain the excesses of democracy. Perry Miller, *The Life of the Mind in America* (New York: Harcourt, 1965), provides the intellectual framework Fredrickson uses. The reference to "thinking like a lawyer" is my own. William McFeeley, *Grant: A Biography* (New York: Norton, 1981), describes Grant as fearful of sliding back into obscurity. Lincoln had the legal profession as a safety net.

11. Basler, ed., *Collected Works,* 2: 320–23 (August 24, 1855).

12. Ibid.; Jacobsohn, "Abraham Lincoln 'On This Question of Judicial Authority,'" 52–70; Basler, ed., *Collected Works,* 4: 2–7 (March 5, 1860).

13. Basler, ed., *Collected Works,* 2: 398–410 (June 26, 1857).

14. Ibid., 4: 168–69 (ca. January 1861).

15. Ibid., 2: 398–410.

16. Ibid., pp. 247–83 (October 16, 1854).

17. White, *When Words Lose Their Meaning,* pp. 3–23.

18. See Jacobsohn, "Abraham Lincoln 'On This Question of Judicial Authority,'" and John Hart Ely, *Democracy and Distrust: A Theory of Judicial Review* (Cambridge, Mass.: Harvard University Press, 1980), for conflicting discussions of the meaning of the process of constitutional debate as it relates to judicial review.

19. Jerome Frank, *Courts on Trial* (Princeton: Princeton University Press, 1949). Legal reasoning is built on several assumptions that arise from its history. In the Jacksonian age it was a means to bring order to an apparently disorderly society. See Miller, *Life of the Mind*. When Christopher Langdell introduced the case method into Harvard, he adopted a scientific method resting on the idea that critical inquiry could discover the principles of law. When the legal realists attacked Langdell's ideas, they did not give up believing that the truth could be found. They insisted not that reality could not be found but that Langdell looked in the wrong place. See Wilfred Rumble, *American Legal Realism: Skepticism, Reform, and the Judicial Process* (Ithaca: Cornell University Press, 1968). The composite of these legal paths rarely has produced modesty as the foundation for the legal perspective. Fuller, *Morality of Law*, pp. 39–40, 193–95, 220–24, and "Human Interaction and the Law," *American Journal of Jurisprudence* 14 (1969): 1–36, notes how much of legal practice and thought rests on cooperation rather than confrontation. Nevertheless, public legal argument is adversarial and creates a binary picture of the world. Lawyers at their best recognize that the method of arguing from precedent to new cases means that understanding a legal principle is an unfolding process. See Edward H. Levi, *An Introduction to Legal Reasoning* (Chicago: University of Chicago Press, 1948). But as they prepare an individual case, lawyers do not claim they are affirming a position that can be expected to outlive its usefulness later. They argue to win, and thus they argue to affirm the truth of their client's position. Even when lawyers ask questions, they do so not to leave the conversation open but to provide the right answer. The overall point is that lawyers adopt an approach to understanding experience which Gadamer challenges for its premises of "the willful domination of existants." He says, "The concept of knowledge based on scientific procedures tolerates no restriction of its claim to universality" (quoted in Weinsheimer, *Gadamer's Hermeneutics*, p. 8).

20. Barber, *On What the Constitution Means*, pp. 34–37.

21. For the Burkean quality of Douglas's argument, see Jean Baker, *Affairs of Party* (Ithaca: Cornell University Press, 1983), pp. 187–90. The Burkean element in Lincoln's thought is suggested in Alexander M. Bickel, *The Least Dangerous Branch: The Supreme Court at the Bar of Politics* (Indianapolis: Bobbs-Merrill, 1962); Edward Pessen, *Jacksonian America: Society, Personality, and Politics* (Homewood, Ill.: Dorsey Press, 1969); and Leonard Richards, "The Jacksonians and Slavery," in Lewis Perry and Michael Fellman, eds., *Antislavery Reconsidered: New Perspectives on the Abolitionists* (Baton Rouge: Louisiana State University Press, 1979), pp. 99–118. I borrow Philip Bobbitt's phrase in *Constitutional Fate: Theory of the Constitution* (New York: Oxford University Press, 1982).

22. Phillip S. Paludan, *A Covenant with Death: The Constitution, Law and Equality in the Civil War Era* (Urbana: University of Illinois Press, 1975); Belz, "Lincoln and the Constitution"; Harold Hyman and William Wiecek, *Equal Justice under Law: Constitutional Development, 1835–1875* (New York: Harper & Row, 1982), pp. 238–41.

23. Paul Finkelman, "The Nationalization of Slavery: A Counterfactual Approach to the 1860s," *Louisiana Studies* 14 (1975): 213–40; Herman J. Belz, *The American Constitution* (New York: Norton, 1983), pp. 286–87; Hyman and Wiecek, *Equal Justice under Law,* pp. 194–95; Don Fehrenbacher, *The Dred Scott Case: Its Significance in American Law and Politics* (New York: Oxford University Press, 1978), chap. 21. A conspiracy is a knowing agreement by a group of individuals to commit a crime. In a political sense, it is an effort to subvert the government through secret means. Nothing in the historical record suggests that Douglas conspired in either sense with his alleged coconspirators. Furthermore, Lincoln's nurturing of public fear that slavery might expand into free states suggests that he recognized the powerful sense of outrage in the North against such action. Whatever may be said about the extent to which *Barron* v. *Baltimore* was known in the late 1850s (a major element in justifying Lincoln's argument), the case would certainly have been well known if there had been any effort to force slavery into free states. A judicial decision to bring slavery into unwilling northern states would have required that Taney's court, in the aftermath of outrage over *Dred Scott,* reverse *Barron,* thus potentially nationalizing the Bill of Rights. Federal judges, appointed by northern-dominated presidents and legislators, would thus control questions of free press, speech, assembly, and petition and the judicial process in Dixie. In the North, judges favoring slavery would face public outrage that would make judicial decisions into occasions for at least disobedience and probably full-scale violence. Douglas's Freeport answer would surely have been confirmed in thunder in that circumstance.

24. Frank Klement, *Dark Lanterns: Secret Political Societies, Conspiracies, and Treason Trials in the Civil War* (Baton Rouge: Louisiana State University Press, 1984); Craig D. Tenney, "Major General A. E. Burnside and the First Amendment: A Case Study of Civil War Freedom of Expression" (Ph.D. dissertation, Indiana University, 1977).

25. Basler, ed., *Collected Works,* 4: 260–69, 300–306 (June 12, 1863); June 29, 1863).

26. Paludan, *Covenant with Death,* pp. 130–32, 141–44; *Harper's Weekly* 7 (1863): 338; Lorraine A. Williams, "Northern Intellectual Reaction to Military Rule during the Civil War," *Historian* 27 (1965): 337–55.

27. Belz, "Lincoln and the Constitution," argues that Lincoln was not a dicta-

tor: the concept is inappropriate in the first place and, when viewed in terms of the overall system and not of narrow legalistic provisions within the document, Lincoln respected the Constitution, rather than threatening it. But Belz does not discuss the Vallandigham case and fails to note the extremes of Lincoln's justifications.

28. Both White, *Heracles' Bow,* pp. 3–27, and Jaffa, *Crisis of the House Divided,* speak of using story to establish new directions for peoples locked in an argument.

29. Quoted in Emory Thomas, *The Confederate Nation* (New York: Harper & Row, 1979), p. 27.

30. I am indebted to Professor Michael Douderoff of the Spanish Department, University of Kansas, for the thought about metaphor distinguishing argument and discussion from storytelling.

31. Basler, ed., *Collected Works,* 5: 346 (July 28, 1862).

CHAPTER FOUR

★

LINCOLN AND OTHER

ANTISLAVERY LAWYERS:

THE THIRTEENTH AND FOURTEENTH

AMENDMENTS AND REPUBLICANS'

POLITICAL AGENDAS

★

HAROLD M. HYMAN

In selecting heroes, people expose their ideas about history. In selecting agendas of controversial public issues, authorities reveal their fears for their present, aspirations for their future, and illusions about their past.[1]

The Constitution's Fourteenth Amendment, written in 1866, was high on President Ronald Reagan's agenda. His federal judicial appointments and Attorney General Edwin Meese's pronouncements that the intentions of the Constitution's framers of 1787 form "the only reliable guide for interpretation" and that the Fourteenth Amendment was never intended to incorporate the federal Bill of Rights against the states reflected the Reagan administration's highest domestic priority. It was to return the Fourteenth Amendment to its pre-1954 somnolence that was seemingly ended in (*Brown* v. *Board of Education*) that year, concerning a federal duty to protect citizens against states' unequal acts or failures to act in Bill of Rights matters.[2]

Meese's suggestions stirred up a still-swirling storm, one given even more passion by Reagan's appointments and nominations to the federal courts. Supreme Court Justice William Brennan characterized the attorney general's views as "little more than arrogance cloaked as humility." Former Justice Arthur Goldberg suggested that Meese aimed less at ascertaining the intentions of the 1787 framers than at the Constitution as altered in 1865 by the Thirteenth Amendment and in 1868 by the Fourteenth, amendments so belatedly implemented by the Supreme Court in 1954.[3]

This recurringly resurfacing argument resembles ancient "strict-construction versus loose-construction" constitutional debates about public policies and recent "creationist versus evolutionary" disputes concerning theology versus science in school curricula. This is not to suggest that the present argument is unimportant because it is either old or current. Rather, it is to stress that individuals' intentions, whether of 1787 or 1868, are extraordinarily difficult for historians confidently to resurrect, and that, unlike many lawyers, few historians do so save in highly restrained terms.

Instead, usually rejecting ideological precommitments, historians tend slowly and incrementally to build mosaiclike estimates, including those about constitution makers' intentions. These accreting estimates allow relatively modest newer looks at old data and justify searches for new sources and perspectives.

One of these new searches is into the history of the nineteenth-century legal profession. Lawyers were the most numerous occupational group who drafted and implemented the Civil War amendments, and jurists and law writers became the amendments' primary interpreters. Unlike today, in the mid-nineteenth century when the Thirteenth and Fourteenth amendments were created, lawyers were popular heroes. One attorney, Abraham Lincoln, then and ever since has stood first in all popular and academic lists of America's heroes. Lincoln shared his eminence with a nonhuman "hero," the 1787 Constitution. It enjoyed star billing in part because generations of Americans likened the Constitution to "a machine that would go of itself."[4]

But the tiny number of pre–Civil War antislavery extension and abolitionist lawyers of Lincoln's generation perceived the constitutional machine as anything but mobile. The unanticipatable motion of the 1860s, toward enhanced "freeitude," measures the frustrations that antislavery lawyers suffered during the 1820–60 decades when the nation, responding to different, southern-accented constitutional drummers, dutifully expanded servitude. But these unending frustrations prepared lawyer-abolitionists who persevered, with ready convictions that in 1861 were appropriate for use in the suddenly dynamic environment of the Civil War.[5]

These convictions were that the framers were part of the Revolution's democratizing continuum that built on the 1776 Declaration of Independence. Then, in the Constitution and Bill of Rights, the framers sketched an evolutionary, dynamic, "organic" national union of states, in which nation and states possessed rights and duties both to each other and to the citizens of each. Preeminent among state duties was the provision of equal legal rights to all state citizens, who by James Madison's formulation were also federal citizens. But the states, especially but by no means only the slave states, at best paid only lip service to this supposedly preeminent state duty, and the new nation did little or nothing about the omissions. Instead, as in the first Judiciary Act under the new Constitution and in suppressing the Whiskey Rebellion, the national government paid attention to the interstate commercial rivalries and the intrastate weaknesses that had inspired the Philadelphia Convention.

Thereafter, commercial law, admiralty, and patent decisions of the Supreme Court's John Marshall–Roger Taney decades (1801–64) attested to the services the Constitution and its implementing judiciary acts provided shippers, investors, inventors, and other mobile risk-takers. Despite or because of its imperfections, the Constitution performed a stabilizing role in large part because of the exploitation of check-and-balance clauses by creative presidents, congressmen, and jurists. Extraconstitutional institutions, especially statewide political parties, and elastic constitutional doctrines accommodated the Louisiana

Purchase, *Marbury, Dartmouth College,* and Henry Clay's American System. In short, adaptive nation-state relationships and shifting balances in the not-too-separated branches of the national government made the Constitution work and were possible under its terms.

By these antislavery perceptions, the greatest success of the Constitution was a series of access laws, of which the Northwest Ordinance and its implementing statutes were preeminent. Like federalism, the ordinance was immediately available for the framers. Breaking through Europe's hierarchically fixed colonial habits, the ordinance encouraged national territories to become states equal to all others, with orderly land surveys, courts, and public schools, and without slavery (a prohibition Congress dropped when forming states in southwestern areas). Granting all sordid speculations, the ordinance was singularly effective social engineering. It helped quickly to populate vast areas with small landholders who became the derivative states' voters—a process often injurious to displaced Indians. Military veterans merged into the mass of settlers, thus avoiding a feared martial class. The diffused landholdings more than ever linked state citizens to both their state and nation, fostering the notion that allegiance required protection. And all that federal and state government had to do was survey and sell the land and provide forums in which free men would protect themselves—schools, courts, post offices, and balloting facilities.[6]

This experience meant that most white Americans at least partially accepted long-developing, evolutionary constitutional notions of abolitionist jurisprudence. But antislavery legalists determined that the 1787 Constitution's arrangements for federalism were nevertheless defective because of slavery. To antislavery lawyers, "freedom national" was not merely mobility as defined in the 1823 *Corfield* v. *Coryell* opinion,[7] but infinitely numerous, practical, homely workaday rights of access, as to education, tramcars, taverns, courts, schools, and jury service, as well as to property, including labor, land, and legal remedies for all rights such as the ballot.

So defined, freedom national visions enhanced state-centered federalism and mixed morality and utility, to use Louis Gerteis's perception. As in the Northwest Ordinance and, seventy years later, the wartime Homestead and Morrill acts (as, indeed, in all Reconstruction efforts including military Reconstruction), freedom national led to more, not fewer, states and self-defending state voters. Thus in 1865 the Thirteenth Amendment, terminating the three-fifths clause, enlarged the number of southern states' representatives. States would continue to make their citizens' civil and criminal relationships as diverse as states' voters and lawmakers wished them to be.

The new measure of national freedom was more uniform, prejudice-free access to intrastate justice, defined in broadest terms to mean the whole unlimitable agenda of life and labor. Equal state protection for persons and property through courts and votes would be the federal duty, a duty the Thirteenth Amendment imposed on every American, whether official or private citizen.[8]

Antislavery legalists justified this states'-rights nationalist vision from eclectic, contextual sources ranging from the Declaration of Independence to the Northwest Ordinance; from equity and *Coryell;* from liberalizing recent history to the nation's duty to protect military veterans who exhibited allegiance; and from the enormities slavery and race prejudice exhibited in the slave and black codes and in community customs.[9] Repeating James Madison's argument in *Federalist* 46 that under the proposed Constitution national and state officials would "resist and frustrate the measures of each other," antislavery lawyers noted that, though acknowledging the state bias of his countrymen, in *Federalist* 51 Madison had hoped that the new federal authority would actively protect individuals' rights against unfairnesses perpetrated by any authorities, state or national, and, by implication, by nonofficials enjoying official sanction. In Virginia's ratifying campaign Madison had failed to win amendments applicable against nation and states. The best that could be done was what became the Ninth Amendment, so long forgotten: "The numeration in the Constitution, of certain rights, shall not be construed to deny or disparage others retained by the people."

Denying that the Ninth Amendment was a mere truism, antislavery legalists saw it instead as a stipulation that every official of nation, state, and locality owed a duty to safeguard individuals' equal rights. Madison's insistence on the Ninth Amendment even as a half-loaf justified arguments that its supporters envisaged incorporating the Declaration of Independence, an argument that abolitionist legalists revived about the Thirteenth and, in turn, Fourteenth amendments. They saw the

Ninth and Thirteenth amendments as commanding not only all authorities but also private offenders.[10]

The antislavery champions perceived correctly that injustices occurred overwhelmingly at the local and state levels, that before 1865 federal justice had been irrelevant as a remedy, and that dual federalism failed for what are now called disfavored persons and groups. The Constitution had faltered most dramatically as state-defined slavery overleaped state boundaries. Slave state spokesmen and their free state coadjutors had long demanded and received extraterritorial protection in the free states and in the future states, the federal territories. *Dred Scott* had made clear that, notwithstanding the Northwest Ordinance and free states' personal liberty laws after *Prigg* v. *Pennsylvania,* this was an increasingly distorted federal union in which the slave states were more equal than others.[11]

In the pre–Civil War Union, federal law required recapture of alleged runaway slaves and returning them to their owners even across state lines without federal or state due process, though the return violated host states' criminal laws against kidnapping, assault, or burglary. In effect, the federal Constitution allowed the property laws of a slave state to apply in a free state, resulting in the seizure and removal of unwilling residents without extradition or other process, to be subject in another state to punishment and even permanent slavery. Further, white or black residents of free states who aided runaways or otherwise obstructed the federal recapture officials, were liable to prosecution, a concern that generated pioneering defenses of individuals' civil rights and liberties.

In striking contrast to the slave states' advantages, the laws and procedures of the free states were not effective in slave states. Massachusetts or Illinois could not affect South Carolina's internal policies on slavery. Free staters could only obey or circumvent the federal Fugitive Slave Law, the latter by enacting state "personal liberty" laws that pitted state law against federal law, and by electing congressmen pledged to oppose extension of slavery into the territories.

But in Congress the three-fifths clause had given slave states a substantial overrepresentation so there was no way ordinary politics could change these distorted arrangements. This imbalance helps to explain why, between the 1790s and the 1850s, although the Northwest Ordinance barred that territory to slave property, the much larger areas dealt with in the misnamed "compromises" of 1820, 1850, and 1854 were successively opened to slavery. Slave territory became slave states, thus perpetuating the sectional imbalance. The Supreme Court's 1857 *Dred Scott* decision escalated the imbalance by its declaration that the nation lacked constitutional authority to *exclude* a state-defined private property from the federal territories. Instead, the Fifth Amendment (part of the Bill of Rights) imposed a duty on the federal government to *protect* slave property there.

There was no easy way to end the nightmare and redress the sectional imbalance. It appeared that continental federalism and state-defined private property were incompatible with political democracy, a fear that helps explain the recurring prominence of the fugitive slave and territorial issues from 1820 to 1860, the very decades when Lincoln, who was born in 1809, committed himself to both lawyering and politics.

To encourage a nobler Union, abolitionist theorists stressed the virtues not of centralization but of a purified state-based federalism in which individuals' state-defined rights, not states' rights, were paramount. They resurrected a generation's memories of the Virginia and Kentucky Resolutions and even of arguments in the 1814 Hartford Convention and South Carolina's 1833 nullification of the federal tariff that justified obstruction of allegedly unconstitutional federal processes. Antislavery lawyers praised state judges who obstructed federal judgments on recalcitrant militiamen in the War of 1812 and protected fugitive slaves and their rescuers between 1820 and 1860, explaining to laymen how state habeas corpus writs could wrest prisoners from federal custody and how juries, obeying instructions from state judges, might decide against federal officers in damage suits.[12]

All these experiences taught that some of the Constitution's clauses were illusory. As an example, the Constitution afforded the nation ultimate military remedies, but only the Civil War unleashed that power in states. Except against counterfeiters, bootleggers, pirates, Indians, Mormons, and those who aided runaway slaves or threatened slave states, until 1861 the federal military expedient was largely theoretical. The minuscule force of regulars was divided into tiny coast-defense garrisons and Indian-fighting units. Real military power was in the states' organized militias, which served the nation's perceived interests in the Whiskey Rebellion and the War of 1812. The Supreme Court sustained presidential authority to "federalize" militiamen in *Martin* v. *Mott* in 1827.[13] But when a few years after *Mott* South Carolina nullified the federal tariff law, Andrew Jackson dared not risk ordering militiamen against their own state. James Buchanan dithered when Wisconsin judges defied a Supreme Court judgment (*Ableman* v. *Booth*) on fugitive slave recaptures and when all the Deep South's states, unsatisfied even by *Dred Scott,* seceded.

Indeed, few prewar Americans ever saw federal officials except for village postmasters and equally familiar land-sales personnel, who were centers of state political organizations. Except for fugitive slave recaptures, almost all federal policies were almost self-executing, overwhelmingly uncoercive, and unbureaucratized.[14]

Then the Civil War made it seem possible to achieve that more perfect Union which, however partially or imperfectly, institutionalized the aspirations of antislavery lawyers. Mobility (and battlefield endurance) made policy possible, first toward the containment of slavery, then toward its nationwide abolition, and then toward a restored state-centered Union that would be still further improvable as posterity might prescribe.

The Union soldiers Lincoln called "thinking bayonets," many of whom were products of Northwest Ordinance public schools, were so literate as to inspire creation of the world's first military postal service and voted as state citizens in globally unique wartime elections. In effect, these bluecoats (with 120,000 black bluecoats among them by 1865) transformed the wartime Emancipation Proclamation into the Thirteenth Amendment.

Meanwhile, in the midst of the Civil War, Congress enacted the 1862 Homestead and Morrill acts, which provided for small-scale federal land sales and tax support for schools from elementary grades through college for all territories and states. Major habeas corpus–jurisdiction acts beginning in 1863 (others followed until 1875) substantially expanded the jurisdiction of federal courts in appeals from state courts, especially in matters of race prejudice and other alleged unfairnesses. These became as much war aims as the Emancipation Proclamation and the Thirteenth Amendment. Appomattox confirmed them. In the restored Union the nation's duty would be to see that citizens could protect their equal legal rights before the laws of their states of residence, an uncentralizing formula following adequately uniform intrastate rights and interstate diversity.

This vision had evolved spasmodically and unsystematically. Major elements were and are at cross-purposes. The basic question of the 1860s remains in the 1990s: short of distorting the federal system, can the federal government perform its duty to implement individuals' civil rights and liberties, as defined by states of residence, if dominant spokesmen in public office and in myriad localities lack goodwill and obstruct implementation or even forcibly resist?

But our perception of this baffling question derives from hindsight. We know the histories of both the First and the Second Reconstructions. Lacking foreknowledge of intractable tensions, Lincoln's generation of prewar antislavery lawyers groped eagerly and often blindly toward shores only dimly seen, of a better, still federal, biracial America in which citizens of both states and nation cohabited in adequate security of person and property on terms other than master-slave. Such a vision was nonsense in 1860. Appomattox made it reasonable. And the Thirteenth Amendment, and then the Fourteenth, seemed to make it imminent.

It remains to link Lincoln and other pre–Civil War antislavery lawyers more definitely to the post-Appomattox question, now again prominent, whether the framers of the Fourteenth Amendment intended to incorporate the Bill of Rights against the states. This linkage becomes possible through examination of some dilemmas pre–Civil War antislavery lawyers faced.

Two seemingly immovable barriers had long frustrated these lawyers. The first was the state-centered federal system, which antedated and underpinned the 1787 Constitution. The second barrier was Americans' pervasive respect for private property, enshrined in national and states' constitutions and laws and preached about by the rising breed of law academics and legal writers. Nineteenth-century lawyers escalated respect for property to a passion.[15]

In the pre–Civil War constitutional world, before the Thirteenth to Fifteenth amendments, states alone defined all civil, criminal, and political relationships and the status of private property. The Constitution's

Fifth Amendment prohibited federal attacks on private property, as Chief Justice Taney stressed in *Dred Scott*.

A tiny minority in their profession, antislavery lawyers had long been distressed and frustrated by their professional commitments favoring state-based federalism and state-defined private property. They struggled with the question of how to oppose slavery and still hold to these treasured essential rights.

Somehow, without conferences or other sharing of insights, Lincoln and other lawyers had weighed this question many times in the pre-1860 decades. By coincidence, Lincoln and three other attorneys, Salmon Portland Chase, Edwin M. Stanton, and William Whiting, began defining ways to help the union of states survive and yet allow federal minima of rights to coexist with state diversity. The result of their approach was to elevate the aims of the Civil War from simply crushing a rebellion to remedying the dangerously unstable prewar situation involving state-centered federalism and individuals' civil—that is, property—rights and civil liberties.

The Illinoisan, Lincoln, the Ohioans Chase and Stanton (the last settled in Pennsylvania), and the Bay Stater, Whiting, were all born between 1808 and 1814. Lincoln, Chase, and Stanton were reared in the intensely racist Ohio River Valley states in which the antislavery provisions of the 1787 Northwest Ordinance applied. In social origins, initial class identification, and legal training, the three midwesterners and Whiting were as different from each other as was possible in white Jacksonian America.

Chase's genealogy, Dartmouth College education, and formal law preparation gave him elite status, a height shared by Whiting, a Back Bay Brahmin and Harvard Law graduate. Stanton attended Kenyon College but did not graduate. His professional training, less systematic than Chase's or Whiting's, put him initially in the middling legal ranks. And Lincoln's mudsill origins and haphazard self-education started him on low rungs. But all four quickly became consummately successful practicing lawyers. Initially, each welcomed all manner of state and local civil and criminal cases. As years passed, they scrambled for and won rich rewards from legal service to the commercial, communication, and industrial interests that were changing American life. Each man in his own law practice applied swiftly evolving new doctrines of contract, tort, and equity law. All four young lawyers took a special interest in patents, which gave them unusual involvement in federal law and developed their talents for innovation within continuities. Professional success required quick educability among law practitioners, especially those servicing that novel category of clients, corporations.

Of the quartet, Chase and Whiting alone became pioneer abolitionists in politics. Pioneering on freedom national antislavery frontiers was easiest for Bostonian Whiting but extremely hazardous for Chase, a resident and law practitioner in southward-looking Cincinnati. Until the Civil War, Stanton kept his feelings on these tender matters largely to himself, for he had moved to Pittsburgh and allied himself professionally and politically with that state's Democratic party, an essentially southern-oriented apparatus. Through the 1840s Lincoln, an aspiring Illinois Whig politician and one-term congressman, like Stanton, first avoided the slavery issue. Unlike Stanton, Lincoln openly committed himself to opposing its further extension (but not abolition), a position that drew him into the new Republican organization in the 1850s.

Chance, plus Lincoln's unanticipated ability as president to select effective civilian department heads from among suitors for preferment who shared his perceptions and might come to share his policies, or at least implement them, drew these four disparate lawyers together in high national offices. Lincoln made Chase secretary of the treasury (and in 1864 named him chief justice of the Supreme Court to succeed the unlamented Taney). Stanton became Lincoln's hyperactive and efficient "Mars," the secretary of war. And Whiting became solicitor of the War Department. The quartet joined their insights about American law, history, constitutionalism, and politics and their shared distaste for slavery and the host of matters connected to it. They also contributed their memories of the prewar crises in constitutionalism, politics, and law that slavery had created and their visions of better ways for the nation to travel if it could survive the Civil War.[16]

High in this unsavory roster was a case that in 1861 the United States Supreme Court, its membership unchanged since *Dred Scott,* had docketed, initiated by a southern slaveowner (*Lemmon* v. *New York*), the outcome of which might have required the free states to revise their law codes to favor slave property. The Union victory and the new Thirteenth Amendment ended the reasonable fear that *Dred Scott*'s judicial spinoffs such as *Lemmon* might nationalize slavery in free states as well as the territories. The Thirteenth Amendment was seen also as ensuring access to land, education, and legal remedies that the wartime Congresses had created in the Morrill, Homestead, and Habeas Corpus acts and was expected to be largely self-executing, although its framers had appended an enforcement clause.

Appomattox made the Thirteenth Amendment and all its contextual content such as the Homestead and Morrill acts worth ratifying, especially in light of *Lemmon* and of a proposed constitutional amendment of 1860–61 that would have unamendably forbidden federal intervention against slavery in states where it existed. In the secession winter President-elect Lincoln and other leading Republicans had grudgingly supported that proposed unamendable thirteenth amendment, and three states had ratified. Then it died as officials and voters at last accepted freedom national perceptions and purposes.[17] By early 1865, Lincoln and much of white America had advanced from this dismal depth to public advocacy of "nigger citizenship," which is why John Wilkes Booth killed Lincoln.

In 1865, unamendability was as defunct as *Dred Scott*. These folk nightmares were replaced by visions of a dynamic, more decent, new federalism. Now the victorious, adaptable constitutional society would transform its agricultural and industrial capabilities into casteless prosperity. Much of post-Appomattox Reconstruction involved these visions, and, for champions of race equality under state law, consequent frustrations.

In contrast to the aborted one of 1861, the Thirteenth Amendment of 1865 eradicated slavery nationwide. Further, it forbade "involuntary servitude" everywhere in the restored Union. In the opinion of the cadres of old abolitionist lawyers, including Chase, Stanton, and Whiting (and, arguably, Lincoln), the Thirteenth Amendment applied not only to discriminatory official acts or failures to act but to all private racial discriminations in all legal relationships, including those lawyerlike relationships of landlord-tenant, employer-employee, or common carrier–passenger.

Still further, the assumption of these antislavery lawyers was that the

Thirteenth Amendment embraced not only the federal Bill of Rights as a decalog of positive national duties to individuals but also as minima of state behavior, to which they added the Declaration of Independence as definition of individuals' civil rights and liberties.

Chase, for example, always argued that Lincoln shared the view that the Thirteenth Amendment "incorporated a distinct recognition of the loyal colored men as citizens, entitled to the right of suffrage."[18] In April 1865, Chase pressed this view on Andrew Johnson, the new president. Then and later Johnson disguised his racist views in John Calhoun–like states'-rights constitutionalism and neo-Darwinian racial demagoguery. A year later, the Republican congressional majority that had been elected with Lincoln in 1864 felt impelled by the new president's impediments to the Thirteenth Amendment as implemented by the Freedmen's Bureau and the world's first civil rights laws of 1865 and 1866 to write the Fourteenth Amendment. Still obstructing, and impeached in 1868, Johnson had nevertheless blunted the fragile movement of Union whites toward full equality for blacks. By the mid-1870s, notwithstanding the further addition to the Constitution of the Fifteenth Amendment, the Lincolnian consensus on political rights of mid-1865 had been transformed and degraded.

No one in the Appomattox spring had anticipated Johnson's hardline encouragement of southern whites' race prejudices. Supporters of the Thirteenth Amendment could not know that it would require bureaucratic implementation in the Freedmen's Bureau and the civil rights acts, plus military Reconstruction, plus the Fourteenth and Fifteenth amendments and *their* enforcement laws. Even to many lawyers, nothing was more surprising than the Supreme Court's rise from *Dred Scott* depths to *Slaughterhouse* heights. Instead, a consensus existed in much of the law world of 1865–73 that no one branch of government had a monopoly in defining the Constitution.[19]

Overleaping such sentiments, in 1867 the Court's *Test Oath* decisions reopened licensed professions including the law to recent rebels, though Congress and several states (one of the latter by a clause of its constitution) had barred such entrance. In 1873 the Court's *Slaughterhouse* decision buried the Thirteenth Amendment in the Fourteenth, degrading the former's universal prohibitions against all involuntary servitude in the state-action formula of the latter and illuminating the way to Jim Crow and *Plessy* v. *Ferguson* (1896).

Alternatives existed as in Chief Justice Chase's 1867 *In re Turner* circuit opinion and Justice William Strong's 1871 *Blyew* views in the Supreme Court. But the *Slaughterhouse* majority preferred not to respect actualities, context, or history. Instead, more anxious to preserve what they asserted were the virtues of prewar federalism but unwilling to explore newer frontiers of racially equalized federalism, the *Slaughterhouse* justices created an abstract, ahistorical recent past. Their creation was adversely to affect the daily lives of millions of Americans until the vital center of the next century.[20]

We remain unsure why the law world of the 1870s acquiesced so generally and tenaciously in *Slaughterhouse* doctrines on federalism and implications favoring the primacy of the Supreme Court in redefining and distorting the Thirteenth Amendment and its sequels. Historical context suggests that the answer lies partly in contemporary changes in legal education and organization.

In the 1860s Christopher Columbus Langdell was readying his alterations of law pedagogy. His triumph at Harvard inspired imitations in many private, state, and Morrill Act universities. Law deans conducted astonishingly successful raids on university budgets to imitate Harvard in creating separate law libraries, faculty, and curricula deemed essential for "scientific" professional law. Alert book publishers took notice, and in 1873, the *Slaughterhouse* year, West Publishing began operations, perhaps shaping legal law pedagogy more than law academics shaped publishing.[21] The separate law libraries began to arrange their holdings, especially case reports, in ways peculiar to the law. Other "new" disciplines, including anthropology, economics, political science, and sociology, were coming to be recognized. Along with medicine and other sciences, they found their publications accommodated in universities' central libraries by any of similarly new data-retrieval (i.e., cataloging) systems (the Dewey decimal, Cutter, or Library of Congress). All could have coped with law. But Langdell won separateness for the Harvard law library, and his emulators nationwide imitated that victory. Law libraries created their own retrieval techniques, often in close cooperation with such commercial law publishers as West and Lippincott, and came to require specialist librarians and other staff. As communication with other campus denizens declined, law librarians rarely collected other than technical reports and related titles.[22] The contextual materials that are the stuff of legal history as of all history—the printed and manuscript autobiographies, diaries, letters, course materials, and lower court briefs—were collected unsystematically if at all. For such reasons the histories of law schools and law firms are generally very thin.

Perhaps, as tentative findings suggest, the revamped law schools and law libraries and the invigorated state bar associations encouraged generations of lawyers and state judges to communicate with one another more than before the Civil War. The associations won control of the access roads to practice, requiring both graduation from a new-style law school and then state licensing through the bar association, a function the Supreme Court had blessed in the 1867 *Test Oath* and 1873 *Bradwell* decisions. So armed, between them law deans and bar association officials (the latter employing delegated state powers) excluded from law education and practice generations of white women, black men and women, Catholics, Jews, and other alleged undesirables. Freedom national ideas withered in this legal culture.[23]

The transformation and degradation of the Lincolnian consensus of 1865 was accomplished in part by this still newer breed of law practitioners, academics, and writers who as never before glorified property rights above all others. From *Slaughterhouse* on, they succeeded in limiting the impact of the Reconstruction amendments to official state action—a virtual invitation for bigots to disguise state discrimination with grandfather clauses, white primaries, exclusionary real estate covenants, rigged jury and tax lists, at-large elections and other gerrymanderings, poll taxes, and separate-but-equal hypocrisies.[24]

It was a long century from *Dred Scott* to *Brown* v. *Board of Education*. Efforts by the Reagan administration to reverse *Brown* did not threaten reversion to *Dred Scott*. But need we return to the degrading and corrosive hypocrisy of *Plessy*, that turn-of-this-century separate-but-equal decision? Nothing that I derive from the histories of Lincoln and the other antislavery lawyers, or from our general history, justifies rear-marching at all.

NOTES

1. John A. Schutz and Douglass Adair, eds., *The Spur of Fame: Dialogues of John Adams and Benjamin Rush, 1805–1812* (San Marino, Calif.: Huntington Library, 1966), pp. 94–95.

2. Meese, in *New York Times*, October 23, 1986; *Chronicle of Higher Education,* October 15, 1986, p. 1.

3. Goldberg, in *Houston Post,* February 21, 1986; Philip Kurland, "Of Meese and (Nine Old) Men," *University of Chicago Law Record* (1986), p. 3.

4. Michael Kammen, *A Machine That Would Go of Itself: The Constitution in American Culture* (New York: Knopf, 1986).

5. Paul Finkelman, "Prelude to the 14th Amendment: Black Legal Rights in the Antebellum North," *Rutgers Law Review* 17 (1986): 415.

6. Peter Onuf, "From Constitution to Higher Law: The Reinterpretation of the Northwest Ordinance," *Ohio History* 94 (1985): 32; Harold M. Hyman, *American Singularity: The 1787 Northwest Ordinance, the 1862 Homestead and Morrill Acts, and the 1944 G.I. Bill* (Athens: University of Georgia Press, 1986), chaps. 1–2.

7. Later, rights to property including licensed professions or trades as in the 1867 *Test Oath* cases and 1873 decisions were embraced as due to national citizens.

8. Louis Gerteis, *Morality and Utility in American Antislavery Reform* (Chapel Hill: University of North Carolina Press, 1987), chaps. 1–6; William Wiecek, *The Sources of Antislavery Constitutionalism in America, 1760–1848* (Ithaca: Cornell University Press, 1977).

9. David Bodenhamer and James W. Ely, eds., *Ambivalent Legacy: A Legal History of the South* (Jackson: University Press of Mississippi, 1984), passim.

10. Jordan Paust, "Human Rights and the Ninth Amendment," *Cornell Law Review* 60 (1975): 231 (n. 22 for Black); A. E. Dick Howard, "Madison and the Constitution," *Wilson Quarterly* 9 (1985): 80.

11. Paul Finkelman, "*Prigg v. Pennsylvania* and Northern State Courts: Anti-Slavery Use of a Pro-Slavery Decision," *Civil War History* 25 (1979): 5.

12. William F. Duker, *A Constitutional History of Habeas Corpus* (Westport, Conn.: Greenwood Press, 1980), pp. 126–35; Charles Warren, "Legislative and Judicial Attacks on the Supreme Court of the United States," *American Law Review* 47 (1913): 1.

13. Lawrence D. Cress, "Citizens in Arms: The Army and the Militia in American Society to the War of 1812" (Ph.D. dissertation, University of North Carolina, 1982).

14. William E. Nelson, *The Roots of American Bureaucracy, 1830–1900* (Cambridge, Mass.: Harvard University Press, 1982), chaps. 1–3.

15. Harold M. Hyman, *A More Perfect Union: The Impact of the Civil War and Reconstruction on the Constitution* (New York: Knopf, 1975), pp. 435–40; Harold M. Hyman and William Wiecek, *Equal Justice under Law: Constitutional Development, 1835–1875* (New York: Harper & Row, 1982), chaps. 7–11.

16. Charles A. Banker, "Salmon P. Chase: Legal Counsel for Fugitive Slaves: Antislavery Ideology as a Lawyer's Creation" (M.A. thesis, Rice University, 1986).

17. Hyman and Wiecek, *Equal Justice under Law*, pp. 192–95 and chaps. 1–10; Paul Finkelman, "The Nationalization of Slavery: A Counterfactual Approach to the 1860s," *Louisiana Studies* 14 (1975): 213.

18. David H. Donald, ed., *Inside Lincoln's Cabinet: The Civil War Diaries of Salmon Portland Chase* (New York: Longmans, Green, 1954), p. 271.

19. Robert J. Kaczorowski, *The Politics of Judicial Interpretation: The Federal Courts, Department of Justice, and Civil Rights, 1866–1876* (Dobbs Ferry, N.Y.: Oceana Publications, 1985), chap. 1.

20. Raoul Berger, "The Fourteenth Amendment: Light from the Fifteenth," *Northwestern University Law Review* 74 (1979): 311; Robert C. Palmer, "Parameters of Constitutional Reconstruction: *Slaughterhouse, Cruikshank,* and the Fifteenth Amendment," *University of Illinois Law Review* (1984): 739–70; Michael L. Benedict, "Preserving Federalism: Reconstruction and the Waite Court," *Supreme Court Review* (1978): 39–79; Hyman and Wiecek, *Equal Justice under Law*, chap. 11.

21. Betty W. Taylor and Robert Munro, eds., *American Law Publishing, 1860–1900,* 4 vols. (Dobbs Ferry, N.Y.: Glanville Publications, 1984–86), a source collection, pioneers this subject.

22. Eliot Freidson, *Professional Powers: A Study of the Institutionalization of Formal Knowledge* (Chicago: University of Chicago Press, 1986).

23. Robert Stevens, *Law School: Legal Education in America from the 1850s to the 1950s* (Chapel Hill: University of North Carolina Press, 1983), chaps. 1–4; Peter Harris, "Ecology and Culture in the Communication of Precedent among State Supreme Courts, 1870–1970," *Law and Society Review* 9 (1985): 449; L. S. Zacharias, "Local Power and Local Knowledge," *American Journal of Legal History* 30 (1986): 122; Charles McCurdy, "Legal Institutions, Constitutional Theory, and the Tragedy of Reconstruction," *Reviews in American History* 4 (1976): 203.

24. Robert J. Kaczorowski, "To Begin the Nation Anew: Congress, Citizenship, and Civil Rights after the Civil War," *American Historical Review* 92 (1987): 45; Patricia Allan Lucie, *Freedom and Federalism: Congress and Courts, 1861–1866*

(New York: Garland, 1986); Earl M. Maltz, "'Separate but Equal' and the Law of Common Carriers in the Era of the Fourteenth Amendment," *Rutgers Law Journal* 17 (1986): 553; Maltz, "Reconstruction without Revolution: Republican Civil Rights Theory in the Era of the Fourteenth Amendment," *Houston Law Review* 24 (1987): 221; William E. Nelson, *The Fourteenth Amendment: From Political Principle to Judicial Doctrine* (Cambridge, Mass.: Harvard University Press, 1988), chaps. 1, 6–8.

CHAPTER FIVE

★

ABRAHAM LINCOLN

AND ANDREW JOHNSON:

A COMPARISON

★

HANS L. TREFOUSSE

On the evening of April 11, 1865, a large number of people had assembled on the White House lawn. The crowd was in a festive mood. The Confederate Army of Northern Virginia had surrendered, and the end of the war was in sight. The elated audience had come to hear the president of the United States deliver a speech.

As the tall, lanky figure began what was to be his last public discourse, the crowd listened with eager anticipation. "We meet this evening," Abraham Lincoln said, "not in sorrow, but in gladness of heart." Then he went on to talk about the problem of reconstructing the southern states, particularly Louisiana, where his own Ten Percent Plan had been put into operation. A state government had been set up and slavery abolished, but Congress had not yet recognized the new regime. He quickly came to the crux of the matter, the number of voters participating in the new government and particularly the problem of black suffrage. "The amount of constituency, so to speak, on which the Louisiana Government rests," he continued, "would be more satisfactory to all if it contained fifty thousand, or thirty thousand, or even twenty thousand, instead of twelve thousand, as it does. It is also unsatisfactory to some that the elective franchise is not given to the colored man. I would myself prefer that it were now conferred on the very intelligent and on those who serve our cause as soldiers."[1]

Lincoln's remarks did not seem particularly exciting, but one of the listeners, the actor John Wilkes Booth, was horrified. "That means nigger citizenship," he said to his companion, David Herold. "Now by God I'll put him through." Vowing that this was the last speech Lincoln would ever deliver, Booth walked away, and three days later at Ford's Theater carried out his infamous plan to murder the president.[2]

The result of Booth's crime was to make Andrew Johnson president, and, considering that the assassin was determined to keep the South a "white man's country," he was quite successful. At first, though, this outcome was not so clear.

Comparisons have often been made between Lincoln and Johnson, and the similarities between the two men have been emphasized.[3] Both were poor whites born in the South; both were firm Unionists; and both seemed to show a great deal of compassion for the conquered section, Lincoln with his Ten Percent Plan and Johnson with his Amnesty and North Carolina proclamations. Nevertheless, these superficial similarities were overshadowed by far more substantial differences.

It is, of course, true that both Lincoln and Johnson experienced hardship in their youth and that neither had promising beginnings. From the start, however, Lincoln sought to overcome his handicaps by forgetting them, by raising himself in the social scale, and by becoming part of the professional elite that was influential in the Illinois state capital he chose as his home. After his well-known humble beginnings and his stints as storekeeper, postal clerk, and boatman, he studied law, settled in Springfield to establish a practice, and married the sister-in-law of one of the most prominent lawyers in town. His practice gave him a good income, and although he had served a few terms in the state legislature and even represented the district for one term in Congress, it was the law, not politics, which until 1854 occupied most of his time. In the meanwhile, virtually cutting off his parents, he did not visit his father before the elder Lincoln died and did not attend the funeral. One thing is certain. Although he never denied his humble beginnings, he took no special pride in them, not even when in 1854, 1855, 1858, and 1860, he sought public office. It was not he but the party that popularized his earlier feats as a rail splitter.[4]

Johnson was entirely different. He too sought to escape from his poor beginnings, which, in many ways, were much worse than Lincoln's. After all, the Emancipator was not apprenticed to a tailor before he had reached his fifteenth birthday, nor did he have the experience of running away from his employer, who advertised for his recapture. When Johnson settled in Greeneville, Tennessee, he continued to practice his trade and never became intimate with the local gentry. On the contrary, proud of his origins, which he rarely failed to mention, he married the daughter of a shoemaker's widow and in his many public offices became the mechanics' spokesman. He turned to full-time politics much earlier than Lincoln, going to the legislature after several years of service as alderman and mayor of Greeneville. Between 1835 and the time he became vice-president, he held public office continuously except for one term, first as a member of the legislature, then as a congressman, governor, senator, and military governor of Tennessee. For all practical purposes, he gave up his private business and supplemented his income with real estate transactions. During all these years, he frequently reminded people of his humble origins and made political capital of his rise from obscurity.[5]

Another great difference was the two presidents' political outlook. Lincoln was a Whig, at least for as long as the party existed, and then he became a Republican. Revering Henry Clay as his political idol, he equally admired Clay's American System. Banks, tariffs, internal improvements, and government aid to industry all found favor with the Springfield lawyer, who at times served as counsel for important railroad corporations. His outlook was shaped by Clay's philosophy, and he never deviated from his conviction of the efficacy of close cooperation between government and industry.[6]

Johnson, in contrast, always abhorred government interference in the economy. Except for an early period of indecision, he was a consistent Democrat, and even in 1864, when he became Lincoln's running mate on the Union party ticket, he ran as a representative of the War Democrats, who had joined with their erstwhile antagonists in defense of the Union. He was not an ordinary Democrat but a Jeffersonian-Jacksonian of the strictest sort. The concept of the noble husbandman guided him throughout his political life, and if he included the so-called "mechanics," or independent craftsmen, in this group, it did not mean that he was any more amicably disposed toward the representatives of industry, business, and commerce. Kenneth M. Stampp has called him "the last Jacksonian." It is equally true and even more descriptive to call him a Jeffersonian as well. The old Jeffersonian school of agrarian democracy appealed to him; there is no evidence that he ever really abandoned it.[7]

His opposition to the American System in all its aspects surfaced early in his career. Even before he had fully joined a party, he thundered in the legislature against internal improvements; the railroads, especially, were anathema to him. They put drovers and inns out of business, he said, and he voted against measures for their benefit. In addition, he supported legislation calling for economy in government and opposed all manner of public expenditures. Compensation for state solicitors, additional sums for the lunatic asylum, and even the payment of money to defray the expenses of the session met with his disfavor. Although his antirailroad stance resulted in his defeat, after he unreservedly identified with the Democratic party and returned to the legislature he continued to stand for economy, as little government aid to industry as possible, and opposition to all schemes he considered extravagant.[8] In Congress, he became the principal foe of the Smithsonian Institution. He opposed rivers and harbors bills, salary increases for government clerks, appropriations of money for White House furniture or for monuments to deceased statesmen, and acquisition of James Madison's library. He favored only one form of government largesse. In keeping with his agrarian outlook, he became one of the fathers of the Homestead bill, which, with single-minded passion, he advocated year in and year out.[9]

Still another important difference between the two presidents concerned their performance as executives. As a political leader, Lincoln had no peer. Faced with opposition from the radicals because of his failure to move more rapidly toward emancipation and from the conservatives for the opposite reason, he gradually took steps toward freeing the slaves and striking at exactly the right time. Allowing the radicals to push him forward and the conservatives to pull him back, he proceeded at his own pace, generally in the direction of freedom, a goal with which he fully sympathized. His masterful handling of the cabinet crisis in December 1862 has become proverbial, and in 1864 his triumph in the face of all opposition, first in securing the party's nomination, then in keeping it, and finally in winning the election against the Democrats was truly astounding. Lincoln was adept at handling men. He knew how to attain his objectives, no matter what the opposition.[10]

Johnson did not possess these skills. Although before the war his executive experience has been much more extensive than Lincoln's, in his two terms as governor of Tennessee he had not achieved any great measures dear to his heart. To be sure, the powers of the chief executive of the Volunteer State were strictly limited, but even within these limits Johnson rarely managed to overcome legislative opposition. He liked to take credit for the establishment of a better educational system, but his own agency in this reform was extremely dubious. His efforts at prison reform did not succeed, and other measures he favored suffered a similar fate. When he became the state's military governor during the war, conditions were too abnormal to test his executive skills, but his administration was hampered by setbacks from the start, and it was not until early 1865 that he was able to establish a new civilian government in Tennessee.[11]

The most crucial difference between the two executives, however, concerned the matter of slavery and race. Though born in a slave state, Lincoln disliked the institution from the very beginning. Whether or not he acquired his antipathy for slavery on his trips to New Orleans, as early as 1837 he called attention to himself as one of two legislators in the Illinois House of Representatives to protest resolutions concerning the sanctity of slave property. The document embodying his objections declared that the signers believed the institution of slavery to be "founded on both injustice and bad policy." In 1847–48, he opposed the war with Mexico, and in 1849 he prepared a bill for the abolition of bondage in the District of Columbia. In his famous Peoria Address in 1854, he denounced the zeal for the spread of the institution "because of the monstrous injustice of slavery itself," a position he upheld in countless speeches afterward.[12]

Nor did Lincoln give up his antislavery convictions during the Civil

War. To be sure, he declared that the war was being fought solely to preserve the Union, but he found numerous occasions to give expression to his dislike for slavery. As early as August 1861, he signed the First Confiscation Act freeing slaves used in operations against the federal government, and though he refused to approve John C. Frémont's efforts to free the slaves in Missouri, by December he sought to bring about compensated emancipation in Delaware. In March 1862, he offered terms for similar action in all border states; in April, he signed the bill abolishing slavery in the District of Columbia; in June, with his approval, the territories became free, and in July he signed the Second Confiscation Act making possible the emancipation of the slaves held by rebels. Moreover, by that time, although he had again countermanded a local commander's emancipation order, he decided upon his own policy of ending slavery in areas still in rebellion. He published his preliminary Emancipation Proclamation in September and, in spite of strong pressure, refused to suspend its operation when he issued the final document of January 1, 1863. Even in his often-quoted reply to Horace Greeley's Prayer of Twenty Millions in which he declared that he would save the Union the shortest way under the Constitution, either by freeing all the slaves, some of the slaves, or none of the slaves, he added that his answer reflected his view of his *official* duty and that he intended no modification of his "oft-expressed *personal* wish that all men, everywhere, could be free."[13]

Following the Emancipation Proclamation, he announced that he would neither retract nor modify it, made it a condition of his offer of amnesty, and stated, "If slavery is not wrong, nothing is wrong." He ran for a second term on a platform calling for a constitutional amendment to end the institution once and for all and was instrumental in securing its passage in the House in the winter of 1864–65. His antislavery credentials are hardly in doubt.[14]

Johnson's views were entirely different. A native of one slave state and a lifelong resident of another, he became a slaveholder as soon as he could afford the purchase, acquiring some eight slaves during his lifetime. Throughout his congressional career, he consistently defended the institution, supported the war with Mexico, opposed the Wilmot Proviso, and voted for the Fugitive Slave Law. As he insisted in 1849 in an address at Evans Cross Roads near his home, slavery might be considered one of the principal ingredients of the American political and social system, "a part of the warp and woof which cannot be removed without spoiling the web." In 1850, he asserted that slavery had its foundation and would find its perpetuity in the Union, and the Union would find its continuance in noninterference with slavery.[15] As he explained in a speech at Raleigh near Memphis in 1857, "He regarded the negro here in a state of slavery in a far better condition than the native African at home. His connection with the white man had an elevating tendency, and many of these negroes who had returned to Liberia had relapsed into the barbarous and savage habits of the natives, showing that the negro is an inferior type of man and incapable of advancing in his native country." When he was governor of Tennessee, this conviction did not keep him from sending to Liberia freed slaves in accordance with the laws of the state.[16] In 1860, he supported the candidate of the National Democrats, John C. Breckinridge, who advocated a federal slave code for the territories, and in 1861, he became the cosponsor of the Johnson-Crittenden Resolutions, which declared that the war was not being prosecuted for the purpose "of overthrowing or interfering with the rights or established institutions" of the southern states but to defend and maintain the supremacy of the Constitution and all laws made in pursuance thereof and to preserve the Union and that as soon as these objects were accomplished it ought to cease.[17]

For the first two years of the conflict, Johnson did not change his mind about slavery. In fact, he was instrumental in inducing Lincoln to omit Tennessee from the Emancipation Proclamation. Only when he saw that the institution was standing in the way of victory and decided that it would be advantageous for him to abandon its defense did he come out for emancipation, a policy he pursued starting in mid-1863. He thus became the Union party's choice for vice-president; nevertheless, his conversion to emancipation came very late in his career.[18]

Closely akin to the question of slavery was the problem of race. In this matter, too, the presidents differed materially. To be sure, a great deal of controversy has surrounded Lincoln's views on human equality. In 1968, Lerone Bennett called him a "white supremacist"; in 1974, in a thoughtful article in *Civil War History,* Don Fehrenbacher, writing about the president, labeled the blacks "only his stepchildren," and a few months later, George M. Fredrickson, in the *Journal of Southern History,* argued that the Emancipator considered the Negro "A Man But Not a Brother." Yet as early as 1958, Richard N. Current stressed Lincoln's ability to grow, and a few years ago, La Wanda Cox in her important book *Lincoln and Black Freedom* showed that the president's concern for the uplift of the freedmen was genuine.[19]

It is true that during much of his life Lincoln held racial views that hardly meet the standard of modern anthropology. Usually, however, he expressed these opinions in reply to racist opponents who denigrated the blacks' humanity; his own outlook was even then much more liberal. As early as 1841, he commented about some chained slaves being sold down the river whom he had seen on a boat. Surprised that in spite of their terrible situation they seemed to be able to dance and play games, he commented that God rendered the worst of human conditions tolerable. Lincoln certainly considered blacks human. And though conceding that a black man might not be the equal of a white in color, and perhaps not in many other respects, still, he asserted, "in the right to put into his mouth the bread that his own hands have earned, he is the equal of every other man, white or black." Instead of constantly using the race issue to whip up the electorate, Lincoln deliberately played it down.[20]

During the war, not only did Lincoln move gradually toward emancipation, but he began to raise black troops and by degrees approached a more modern view of racial equality. Although in August 1862, he still invited black leaders to the White House to tell them that colonization was probably the best answer to the race problem in the United States, and although he attempted to carry out such a scheme by settling some blacks at the Île à Vache in Haiti, when the experiment failed, he recalled the surviving settlers. And though he continued to talk about colonization, it is very doubtful that his references to the subject signified anything more than a sop to conservatives. The impossibility of large-scale expatriation of the blacks must have become increasingly clear to him.[21]

In 1864, the Emancipator had moved far beyond most of his countrymen. He was now contemplating the elevation of the freedmen to citizenship. As he put it in a letter to Governor Michael Hahn of Louisiana, "I barely suggest for your private consideration, whether some of the colored people may not be let in [to the suffrage]—as, for instance, the very intelligent, and especially those who have fought gallantly in our ranks. They would help, in some trying time to come, to keep the jewel of liberty within the family of freedom." And though there has been considerable controversy about the authenticity of his famous letter to General James S. Wadsworth, its first two paragraphs at least are generally considered to be genuine. In these, Lincoln declared that if universal amnesty were granted, he could not avoid exacting universal suffrage in return, "or at least suffrage on the basis of intelligence and military service."[22] His public avowal in his last speech of the need for black enfranchisement has already been cited. For a nineteenth-century poor white brought up in slaveholding Kentucky and proslavery southern Indiana, such an attitude was very advanced and exceptional.

Johnson's views on the subject were hardly comparable. Never questioning the "peculiar institution" during his prewar career, he subscribed to the commonly held racist justification for it. He made his stand absolutely clear in the congressional debates about the gag rule. "If one portion of the country were to be masters and the other menial . . . ," he said, "he had no hesitancy in bringing his mind to a conclusion on the subject, believing and knowing, as he did, that the black race of Africa were inferior to the white man in point of intellect—better calculated in physical structure to undergo drudgery and hardship—standing, as they do, many degrees lower in the scale of gradation that expresses the relative relation between God and all that he has created than the white man." Moreover, he continued, if the laws did not distinguish between white and black people, "they would place every splay-footed, bandy-shanked, hump-backed, thick-lipped, flat-nosed, woolly-headed, ebon-colored negro in the country upon an equality with the poor white man." He reiterated similar opinions in other speeches.[23]

Nor did the war change his attitude. To be sure, he finally came out for emancipation; he even promised the blacks that he would be their Moses to lead them to the promised land, but he never abandoned his racist views. As he wrote to General George H. Thomas after he had become president, "I have information of the most reliable character that the negro troops stationed at Greeneville, Tenn. . . . are committing depredations throughout the country, domineering over, and in fact running the white people out of their neighborhood. . . . The negro soldiery take possession of and occupy property in the town at discretion, and have even gone so far as to have taken my own house and converted it into a rendez-vous for male and female negroes, who have congregated there, in fact making it a common negro brothel. It was bad enough to be taken by traitors and converted into a rebel hospital but a negro whore house is infinitely worse." And after an interview with a group of blacks led by Frederick Douglass, to whom he refused to concede the necessity of black suffrage, he turned to his secretary and reputedly said, "Those d——d sons of b——s thought they had me in a trap. I know that d——d Douglass; he's just like any nigger, & he would sooner cut a white man's throat than not."[24] As late as 1868, Johnson complained to his private secretary that blacks and not white laborers were being employed on the White House grounds.[25]

It is true that, like Lincoln, he urged southern governors to enfranchise at least some blacks. But that his interest in expanding the suffrage was not owing to any desire to elevate the freedmen he made perfectly clear in his often-quoted letter to Governor William Sharkey of Mississippi, which contrasts markedly with Lincoln's advice to Hahn. "If you could extend the elective franchise to all persons of color who can read the Constitution of the United States in English and write their names, and to all persons of color who own real estate valued at not less than two hundred and fifty dollars, and pay taxes thereon," Johnson wrote, "you would completely disarm the adversary and set an example the other States will follow. This you can do with perfect safety, and thus place the southern States, in reference to free persons of color, upon the same basis with the free States. I hope and trust your convention will do this, and, as a consequence, the radicals, who are wild upon negro franchise, will be completely foiled in their attempt to keep the southern States from renewing their relations to the Union by not accepting their senators and representatives." Unlike the Emancipator, he was not really interested in the blacks.[26]

Thus the man who succeeded Lincoln in April 1865 had an entirely different outlook from that of his predecessor. This might not have been very significant under normal conditions, but in the spring of 1865, conditions were far from normal. The Civil War was ending, the seceded states had to be brought back into the Union, and, above all, the newly freed blacks had to be integrated into society. The latter problem was the central issue of Reconstruction. Difficult to solve under any circumstances, it required the hand of a master. Lincoln was such a master, and although La Wanda Cox has shown that even he might have had severe problems, at least he probably would have tried.[27] Even at the moment of his assassination, he was modifying his previous policies. These had, after all, been measures devised during wartime; his offers of amnesty and his plans for Reconstruction were designed as much to weaken the enemy by winning over as many Confederates as possible as they were genuine measures of restoration. In consequence, he had already modified his policy toward Virginia, where, a few days earlier, he had offered to let the Confederate legislature meet in order to take the state out of the Confederacy. But on April 9, Robert E. Lee surrendered to Ulysses S. Grant; Lincoln returned home from Richmond and countermanded the order. Not only were many of his advisers, including the radicals, opposed to the scheme, but it was no longer necessary to induce the Confederates to abandon their cause.[28] How he would have proceeded had he lived we cannot know. Shrewd politician that he was, however, it is most likely that he would have seen to it that the supremacy of the Republican party was preserved and that the restoration of the South and the lapse of the three-fifths compromise would not have resulted in a strengthening of the Democratic opposition. The only way to do this was to enfranchise at least some blacks. In view of Lincoln's attitude toward the freedmen, he might well have found a way to do so.

Johnson had no such plans. Although at first he reiterated his conviction that treason must be made infamous and traitors punished, he was certain that legally the states had never seceded and were therefore still in the Union. All that had to be done was to reanimate them. But he did not believe the federal government had any right to meddle with suffrage qualifications. Consequently, with his promulgation of the Amnesty and North Carolina proclamations, he sought to restore them as quickly as possible.[29]

By not moving to exact conditions from the South immediately after the assassination, the new president missed a splendid chance to reshape the defeated section. Stunned by the news of the crime, brought low by the collapse of the Confederacy, and apprehensive about the intentions of the victors, southerners were in a chastened mood. "At the time of the surrender of General Lee's army and the restoration of peace . . . ," testified John Minor Botts before the Reconstruction Committee, "there was, not only a general, but an almost universal, acquiescence and congratulations among the people that the war had terminated, and a large majority of them were at least contented, if not gratified, that it had terminated by a restoration of the State to the Union. And at that time, the leaders, too, seemed to have been entirely subdued . . . and a more humble, unpretending set of gentlemen I never saw than they were at that time." Watkins James, an assessor at Winchester, agreed. At the time of the surrender, he said, the people were "quiet, peaceable, disposed to submit to almost anything." Similar testimony came from the sheriff of Fairfax County, Jonathan Roberts, who recalled that "as soon after the surrender of Lee as the rebels could get home, they all seemed to be perfectly happy with everything."[30]

Similar conditions prevailed in other states. In Alabama, Mailton Sanford remembered, "immediately after the surrender of the Confederate forces, the rebel influence was very much appalled, overthrown, and destroyed there. The rebels were very much subjugated . . . and made strong profession of submission to the government." In North Carolina, Whitelaw Reid heard the editor of the *Raleigh Press* state that he was anxious for reunion, and much as the people hated Negro suffrage, they would even accept that if necessary. In Florida, too, Johnson learned that the great majority of the people were determined to come directly and quickly back in any form he might prescribe, and General George A. Custer observed the same reaction in Texas. As Carl Schurz emphasized in his report at the end of the year, "When news of Lee's and Johnston's surrenders burst upon the Southern country, the general consternation was extreme. . . . The public mind was so despondent that if readmission at some future time under whatever conditions had been promised, it would have been looked upon as a favor."[31]

Johnson, however, waited until May, when he issued his proclamations. Promising amnesty to all but fourteen exempted classes, he called upon the legal voters of North Carolina to elect delegates to a convention to restore the state to the Union. Privately, he suggested that North Carolina ratify the Thirteenth Amendment, repeal the Confederate debt, and nullify the secession ordinance—conditions he also prescribed for other states—but he did not insist on all of these.[32] Too much of a Jeffersonian to interfere effectively in the affairs of individual states, he was too intent on proving his contention that they had never been out of the Union, to say nothing of the fact that he had never been a very efficient executive. The result was that there was a total change in attitude in the South.

Many observers noted this transformation. When Whitelaw Reid arrived in Mobile, he was struck by the difference between the frame of mind there and the impressions he had gained on the Atlantic coast. "There they were just as vehement in their protestations against negro suffrage," he recalled, "but they ended in entreaties that the conquerors would spare the infliction of such disgrace. Here came threats. Everywhere else it was manifest that if the restoration of civil authority would depend upon negro suffrage, then negro suffrage would be accepted. Here, for the first time, we were told that the people would not stand for it! The explanation is simple. They were just beginning to get a knowledge of the North Carolina proclamation, and to imagine that the President was willing to concede to them more power than they had dared to hope. They had been offered an inch; they were soon to be seen clamoring for ells." The journalist J. T. Trowbridge agreed: "The more lenient the government, the more arrogant they became," he wrote of the southerners he observed. In New Orleans, the Louisiana Unionist Justice Rufus Howell took note of a similar trend. "At one time, immediately after the surrender, I think it would have been a pretty close vote . . . ," he testified. "But after the policy of the President began to be understood . . . the old feeling of hatred returned."[33]

There were parallel developments elsewhere. Conservatives were becoming more defiant in Texas, Custer observed, and Thaddeus Stevens heard similar stories from Mississippi. As one of his correspondents explained, "Whatever genuine Unionism was forming and would in time have grown up has been checked by Mr. Johnson's course. He has made a great mistake. He is now the favorite of all the disaffected elements here." Johnson's own appointee, Governor William W. Holden, reported from North Carolina that in May and June, "rebellious spirits would not have dared to show their heads, even for the office of constable; but leniency has emboldened them and the copperhead now shows his fangs." The president heard the same thing from Georgia, learning that before his pardons were granted, political instigators were held in check. As his correspondent put it, "They were all endeavoring to see who could do the most for you and magnifying little acts of courtesy to Union men during the war into great deeds. Now that they all have their pardons they are all on the other track."[34] Confirmation of this news came from Virginia, where Watkins James blamed the leniency of the government for the change, and from Arkansas, where General J. W. Sprague wrote to John Sherman, "For some time after the 'surrender' those who returned from the Rebel armies were the most quiet and orderly. It is not so now." And Johnson's confidential secretary, General Reuben D. Mussey, admitted in October 1865 that "we had the opportunity when Lee surrendered and more than that when Lincoln was assassinated to make our own terms. . . . I fear the opportunity has now been lost." As Christopher Memminger, the former secretary of the treasury of the Confederacy, summed it up in a letter to Carl Schurz, "I think you are right in saying that if we had originally adopted a different course as to the negroes, we would have escaped present difficulties. But if you will consider a moment, you will see that it was as impossible, as for us to have emancipated them before the war. The then President held up before us the hope of a 'white man's government,' and this led us to set aside negro suffrage. We might probably even have procured what was then called 'impartial suffrage,' but it was natural that we should yield to our old prejudices."[35]

Thus the assassination of Abraham Lincoln led to the inauguration of policies which, from the beginning, made any real racial reform impossible. Because Johnson differed from his predecessor in outlook, ideology, and political habits, Booth's assassination of Lincoln to prevent Negro citizenship succeeded at that time. The crime at Ford's Theater was an even greater disaster than was realized at the moment. Some of its effects would not be overcome for another century.

NOTES

1. Roy P. Basler, ed., *The Collected Works of Abraham Lincoln*, 9 vols. (New Brunswick: Rutgers University Press, 1953–55), 8: 399–405.

2. William Hanchett, *The Lincoln Murder Conspiracies* (Urbana: University of Illinois Press, 1983), p. 37; Benjamin Thomas, *Abraham Lincoln* (New York: Knopf, 1952), pp. 514–15.

3. Lately Thomas, *The First President Johnson: The Three Lives of the Seventeenth President of the United States of America* (New York: Morrow, 1968), pp. 7, 49–50; *Washington National Intelligencer*, January 27, 1868.

4. Stephen B. Oates, *With Malice toward None: The Life of Abraham Lincoln* (New York: Harper & Row, 1977), pp. 3–176; Thomas, *Lincoln*, p. 206.

5. James E. Sefton, *Andrew Johnson and the Uses of Constitutional Power* (Boston: Little, Brown, 1980), pp. 1–102; Harriet S. Turner, "Recollections of Andrew Johnson," *Harper's Monthly* 120 (January 1910), pp. 168–76, esp. 169.

6. Gabor S. Boritt, *Lincoln and the Economics of the American Dream* (Memphis: Memphis State University Press, 1978), passim.

7. Thomas Perkins Abernethy, *From Frontier to Plantation in Tennessee: A Study in Frontier Democracy* (Memphis: Memphis State University Press, 1955), p. 320; LeRoy P. Graf and Ralph W. Haskins, eds., *The Papers of Andrew Johnson*, 7 vols. (Knoxville: University of Tennessee Press, 1967–86), 2: 174, 3: 52 (hereafter cited as *PAJ*); Kenneth M. Stampp, *The Era of Reconstruction, 1865–1877* (New York: Knopf, 1965), pp. 50–82.

8. John Brownlow to Oliver P. Temple, September 2, 1891, Oliver P. Temple Papers, University of Tennessee; Oliver P. Temple, *Notable Men of Tennessee, 1833–1875* (New York: Cosmopolitan Press, 1912), pp. 364–68; *Tennessee House Journal*, 21st General Assembly, 1st sess., pp. 357, 463–64, 657, 671, 358, 564, 635, 262; 23d General Assembly, 1st sess., pp. 246, 262, 355, 233, 238–39.

9. *PAJ*, 1: 394–96, 400–403, 468–72, 440, 427–28; *Congressional Globe*, 28th Cong., 2d sess., pp. 330, 369; Benjamin Horace Hibbard, *A History of the Public Land Policies* (New York: Macmillan, 1924), pp. 378–79.

10. Hans L. Trefousse, *The Radical Republicans: Lincoln's Vanguard for Racial Justice* (New York: Knopf, 1969), pp. 203–39, 240–41, 289–97; Oates, *With Malice toward None*, pp. 327–30; William Frank Zornow, *Lincoln and the Party Divided* (Norman: University of Oklahoma Press, 1954), passim.

11. Herbert Blair Bentley, "Andrew Johnson, Governor of Tennessee, 1853–1857" (Ph.D. dissertation, University of Tennessee, 1972), pp. 132–40, 149, 185–86; *PAJ*, 5: li–lii; Peter Maslowski, *Treason Must Be Made Odious: Military Occupation and Wartime Reconstruction in Nashville, Tennessee, 1862–1865* (Millwood, N.Y.: KTO Press, 1978), pp. 21, 34, 146ff.; Temple, *Notable Men*, pp. 406–16.

12. Basler, ed., *Collected Works*, 1: 74–75, 2: 247–83, esp. 255; Oates, *With Malice toward None*, pp. 79–81, 86, 114–18, 127–30, 155–57.

13. Hans L. Trefousse, *Lincoln's Decision for Emancipation* (Philadelphia: Lippincott, 1975), pp. 15–56; Basler, ed., *Collected Works*, 5: 388–89.

14. Basler, ed., *Collected Works*, 7: 81, 54, 281; James G. Randall and Richard N. Current, *Lincoln, the President: Last Full Measure* (New York: Dodd, Mead, 1955), pp. 298–321; La Wanda Cox, *Lincoln and Black Freedom: A Study in Presidential Leadership* (Columbia, S.C.: University of South Carolina Press, 1981), pp. 7–19.

15. *PAJ*, 1: 337–47, 416, 499, 552; *Washington National Intelligencer*, September 14, 1850; David Warren Bowen, "Andrew Johnson and the Negro" (Ph.D. dissertation, University of Tennessee, 1976), pp. 106–7. The exact number of slaves Johnson owned is in dispute.

16. *PAJ*, 2: 477, 360–61, 377–78, 380, 445, 447–48, 450–451.

17. Thomas, *Johnson*, pp. 149–50, 204; *PAJ*, 4: 598.

18. *PAJ*, 6: 85–86, 344–45, 7: 251–53; John Cimprich, *Slavery's End in Tennessee, 1861–1865* (University, Ala.: University of Alabama Press, 1985), p. 462; Sefton, *Johnson*, pp. 94, 98.

19. Lerone Bennett, Jr., "Was Abe Lincoln a White Supremacist?" *Ebony* 23 (February 1968): 37; Don E. Fehrenbacher, "Only His Stepchildren: Lincoln and the Negro," *Civil War History* 20 (1974): 293–310; George M. Fredrickson, "A Man But Not a Brother: Abraham Lincoln and Racial Equality," *Journal of Southern History* 41 (1975): 39–58; Richard N. Current, *The Lincoln Nobody Knows* (New York: Hill and Wang, 1958), pp. 233–36; Cox, *Lincoln and Black Freedom*, pp. 31–139.

20. Basler, ed., *Collected Works*, 1: 260, 2: 520; Cox, *Lincoln and Black Freedom*, pp. 20–22.

21. Trefousse, *Lincoln's Decision for Emancipation*, pp. 42, 45, 54.

22. Basler, ed., *Collected Works*, 7: 243, 101–2; Harold M. Hyman, "Lincoln and Equal Rights for Negroes: The Irrelevancy of the 'Wadsworth Letter,'" *Civil War History* 12 (1966): 258–66.

23. *PAJ*, 1: 136–40, 498–509, 3: 328–29.

24. *PAJ*, 7: 251–53; Johnson to George H. Thomas, September 4, 1865, Andrew Johnson Papers, LC; Philip Ripley to Manton Marble, February 8, 1866, Manton Marble Papers, LC.

25. Diary of Col. William G. Moore, p. 4 (April 9, 1868), Johnson Papers.

26. Edward McPherson, *The Political History of the United States during the Period of Reconstruction, April 15, 1865–July 15, 1870* (Washington, D.C.: Solomons & Chapman, 1871), pp. 19–20.

27. Cox, *Lincoln and Black Freedom*, pp. 142–83.

28. Basler, ed., *Collected Works*, 8: 386–88, 406–8; Randall and Current, *Lincoln*, pp. 353–58.

29. *PAJ*, 7: 576, 583, 506; *New York Times,* August 22, 1865.

30. *Report of the Joint Committee on Reconstruction,* H.R. No. 30, 39th Cong., 1st sess. (Washington, D.C., 1866), pt. 2, pp. 120, 33–34, 41ff. (hereafter cited as *RJCR*).

31. Ibid., pt. 3, p. 60; Whitelaw Reid, *After the War: A Tour of the Southern States, 1865–1866,* ed. C. Vann Woodward (New York: Harper & Row, 1965), p. 44; George Harris to Johnson, May 21, 1865, Johnson Papers; *RJCR,* pt. 4, pp. 72–73; Frederick Bancroft, ed., *Speeches, Correspondence and Political Papers of Carl Schurz,* 6 vols. (New York: G. P. Putnam's Sons, 1913), 1: 282.

32. McPherson, *Reconstruction,* pp. 9–12; Albert Castel, *The Presidency of Andrew Johnson* (Lawrence, Kan.: Regents Press of Kansas, 1979), pp. 44–45.

33. Reid, *After the War,* pp. 219–20; J. T. Trowbridge, *The South: A Tour of Its Battle-Fields and Ruined Cities* (1866; rpt. New York: Arno Press, 1969), p. 189; *New Orleans Riots,* H.R. No. 16, 39th Cong., 2d sess. (Washington, D.C., 1867), p. 50.

34. *RJCR,* pt. 4, pp. 72–73; R. W. Flournoy to Thaddeus Stevens, November 20, 1865, Thaddeus Stevens Papers, LC; W. W. Holden to Johnson, December 6, 1865, F. Y. Clark to Johnson, December 4, 1865, Johnson Papers.

35. *RJCR,* pt. 2, p. 42; J. W. Sprague to John Sherman, April 4, 1866, John Sherman Papers, LC; Frank R. Levstick, "A View from Within: Reuben D. Massey on Andrew Johnson and Reconstruction," *Historical New Hampshire* 27 (1972): 169; Christopher Memminger to Carl Schurz, April 26, 1871, Carl Schurz Papers, LC.

CONCLUSION

★

JOEL H. SILBEY

American politics in the Civil War era, as these chapters strikingly demonstrate, had a full complement of colorful moments, good and bad leaders, and high drama, as well as critical consequences for the nation. Each episode and personal confrontation can be detailed and analyzed, as these authors have effectively done, to illuminate important aspects of the American political scene in the middle of the nineteenth century. Stepping back from the direct focus on these chapters, however, I will conclude this book with a few suggestions regarding larger themes in political history suggested by these essays.

It is unnecessary to discuss the differences over historical methodology that have often preoccupied political historians in recent years. I am sure we can all agree that any method that clarifies, makes concrete, and sharpens understanding is useful and should be utilized when appropriate. Nor will I say anything more about whether the study of politics should be primarily a study of the leadership and policy makers, or should concentrate, rather, on their followers, the voters and others who made up the large majority of the members of the American political nation. In the spirit of ecumenicalism, it is enough to say that many of these chapters open up that topic quite well and illustrate effectively how much political historians can and have usefully considered all levels of the political world and the interaction among them.

Historiographically, we live in an age of political culture. Although historians do not search for national character these days as much as they once did, the nature of our political culture has become a major preoccupation. Historians emphasize the things that link a people together politically, their shared values, memories, and perspectives. Further, when many current scholars talk about political culture, the notion of republicanism seems to be the common denominator. Historians first pinpointed republicanism as the dominating focus of the American political outlook in the late eighteenth and perhaps early nineteenth centuries. Some scholars, however, see the idea persisting well beyond the revolutionary era and its aftermath. It has begun to creep further and further into the nineteenth century with some students of the period believing that it has relevance into the Civil War era.

Every society has a political culture and we should seek to define and understand it at any given moment. In the hands of capable scholars, Joyce Appleby, Richard Buel, Isaac Kramnick, Dorothy Ross, Stephen Watts, and many others, the application of the notion of republicanism to our past politics, evaluating its importance and tracing its rise and fall, can be very illuminating. But we can go too far, I suggest, in one direction in those attempts. I would argue that we should keep clearly in sight the balance between consensual elements uniting Americans— that is, the basics of the general political culture—and the ever-ready possibility, and reality, of sharp divisions between people even as they internalize the same cultural norms. Thus a common political culture can, and in the case of Civil War–era America, did, have numerous sectional, partisan, ethnic, and class divisions.

Michael Holt observed a few years ago that "real and intense differences over issues, values and group antagonisms" existed between political parties and among Americans generally in the middle of the nineteenth century. We must remember that as we seek to understand the era. These differences cannot readily fit within an overarching dominance of republican political values. They exceeded the usual range of divisions within commonly held norms. In the period from the 1830s through the Civil War the American political world was very divisive, not consensual. Republicanism stressed national consensus and abhorred conflict. The partisanship characterizing the middle of the nineteenth century—from Andrew Jackson's and Martin Van Buren's time to Andrew Johnson's and beyond—did neither. Perhaps most Americans did agree somewhat, in a general way, on a set of commonly held political values. But if they did, they searched for republican ends with sharply different perspectives, understandings, and aims, in ways quite distinct from those who strode the political world in an earlier, more republican, time. Mid-nineteenth-century Americans accepted, and made part of their culture, the normality of divisions in society, the persistence of conflict, and the system's organization by collective political institutions, in particular, parties, in ways that earlier citizens, deeply believing in the norms of republicanism and antipartyism, never did, or could.

These chapters also are a lesson in locating and understanding the timing of change and catching the significant turning points in our political past. Political historians have spent much time in recent years considering the adequacies and shortcomings of various chronological organizing schemes for past politics with different dating and turning points—from the presidential synthesis to critical election theory and beyond. For what I have suggested was a partisan political culture, none of the existing schemes quite fits. Moreover, recent generations of economic, diplomatic, and intellectual historians have stopped seeing the Civil War as a major turning point. Political historians should do so as well, I believe.

Whatever Lincoln and Johnson faced and did in the 1860s, both were products of the existing partisan political culture, had grown up within it, understood it in its own terms, and accepted its dictates. The war may have influenced Americans at different political levels in certain ways and may have placed some issues at the forefront that otherwise would not have been. But whatever the Civil War did or did not do, the behavior of America's leaders and its electorate remained rooted in other times and the values and ways of engaging in politics of those times. As the years passed, the memories of the war were to affect the political world more directly and powerfully. But even those events were always rooted in the continuing strength of the earlier forces still at play. In that sense, neither 1860, 1865, nor 1877 was a critical dividing line for the American political nation in values, behavior, norms, or institutions. Such a line would not appear until the 1890s. That Lincoln and Johnson and their colleagues still inhabited the political world originally defined by Andrew Jackson and Martin Van Buren remains a central fact in our full understanding of Civil War politics.

THE CONTRIBUTORS

★

LLOYD E. AMBROSIUS is a professor of history at the University of Nebraska–Lincoln. A specialist in the history of American foreign relations and the American presidency, he is the author of *Woodrow Wilson and the American Diplomatic Tradition: The Treaty Fight in Perspective* (1987) and has served as the Mary Ball Washington Professor of American History at University College, Dublin, Ireland.

THOMAS B. ALEXANDER is an emeritus professor of history at the University of Missouri–Columbia, where he was the Frederick A. Middlebush Professor. His publications include *Political Reconstruction in Tennessee* (1950), *Thomas A. R. Nelson of East Tennessee* (1956), and *Sectional Stress and Party Strength: A Study of Roll-Call Patterns in the United States House of Representatives, 1836–1860* (1967), and he is coauthor of *The Anatomy of the Confederate Congress: A Study of the Influences of Member Characteristics on Legislative Voting Behavior, 1861–1865* (1972), which won the Charles S. Sydnor Award from the Southern Historical Association and the Jefferson Davis Award from the Confederate Memorial Literary Society. He has served as president of the Southern Historical Association and the Social Science History Association.

PHILLIP S. PALUDAN is a professor of history at the University of Kansas. He is the author of *A Covenant with Death: The Constitution, Law and Equality in the Civil War Era* (1975), *Victims: A True Story of the Civil War* (1981), and *"A People's Contest": The Union and the Civil War, 1861–1865* (1988), and has served as a Liberal Arts Fellow at Harvard Law School.

JOHN NIVEN is a professor of history at the Claremont Graduate School. His publications include *Connecticut for the Union* (1965), *Years of Turmoil: The Civil War and Reconstruction* (1969), *Gideon Welles: Lincoln's Secretary of the Navy* (1973), *Connecticut Hero: Israel Putnam* (1977), *Martin Van Buren and the Romantic Era of American Politics*

(1983), *The American President Lines and Its Forebears, 1848–1984: From Paddle Wheelers to Container Ships* (1986), *John C. Calhoun and the Price of Union* (1988), and *The Coming of the Civil War* (1989). His books have won awards from the Pacific Coast Branch of the American Historical Association, the National Association of State and Local History, and the New Haven Civil War Round Table, and the Jules and Frances Landry award.

HAROLD M. HYMAN is the William P. Hobby Professor of American Constitutional and Legal History at Rice University. He is coauthor of *Stanton: The Life and Times of Lincoln's Secretary of War* (1962) and *Equal Justice under Law: Constitutional Development, 1835–1875* (1982) and author of *A More Perfect Union: The Impact of the Civil War and Reconstruction on the Constitution* (1973). His books *Era of the Oath: Northern Loyalty Tests during the Civil War and Reconstruction* (1954) and *To Try Men's Souls: Loyalty Tests in American History* (1959) won the Albert J. Beveridge Award and the Sidney Hillman Foundation Prize.

HANS L. TREFOUSSE is Distinguished Professor of History at Brooklyn College and the Graduate Center of the City University of New York. He is the author of *Germany and American Neutrality, 1939–1941* (1951), *Ben Butler: The South Called Him Beast* (1957), *Benjamin Franklin Wade: Radical Republican from Ohio* (1963), *The Radical Republicans: Lincoln's Vanguard for Racial Justice* (1969), *Impeachment of a President: Andrew Johnson, the Blacks, and Reconstruction* (1975), *Carl Schurz: A Biography* (1981), and *Andrew Johnson: A Biography* (1989). His various honors include a Distinguished Teacher Prize from Brooklyn College and a John Simon Guggenheim Fellowship.

JOEL H. SILBEY is the President White Professor of History at Cornell University. His books include *The Partisan Imperative: Essays on the Dynamics of American Politics before the Civil War* (1985), *A Respectable Minority: The Democratic Party in the Civil War* (1977), *Political Ideology and Voting Behavior in the Age of Jackson* (1973), and *The Shrine of Party: Congressional Voting Behavior, 1841–1852* (1967). He has been a fellow at the Center for Advanced Study in the Behavior Sciences and a visiting scholar at the Russell Sage Foundation.

INDEX